Recognizing an Historic Injustice: Canada's First National Internment Operations, 1914-1920

A unit for secondary students exploring the events, causes and consequences of the internment of thousands of individuals in Canada during the First World War era

PIVOTAL VOICES

Authors

Atul Bahl

Ilan Danjoux

Lindsay Gibson

James Miles

Editors

Atul Bahl

Roland Case

THE CRITICAL THINKING CONSORTIUM

1914-1920

www.internmentcanada.ca

Series published by

The Critical Thinking Consortium
4th Floor – 1580 West Broadway
Vancouver, BC V6J 5K8
Tel: 604.639.6325
Fax: 604.639.6325
E-mail: mail@tc2.ca
Web: www.tc2.ca

Cover Design: Sharlene Eugenio, Pacific Educational Press
Interior Design: M. Kathie Wraight
Production: M. Kathie Wraight
Copyediting: Catherine Edwards
Cover Photographs: **Top:** Whyte Museum of the Canadian Rockies—William D. Buck Fonds.
   Second row: Queen's University Archives, Canadian First World War Internment Recognition Fund.
   Third row: Library and Archives Canada, Glenbow Museum—NA 1870-6, Glenbow Museum—NA 626-19,
   Library and Archives Canada. **Bottom:** Whyte Museum of the Canadian Rockies.

This resource has been made possible by a grant from the Endowment Council of the Canadian First World War
Internment Recognition Fund. We gratefully acknowledge the valuable feedback from our advisory commitee:
Lubomyr Luciuk, Ruth Sandwell and Marsha Skrypuch.

Library and Archives Canada Cataloguing in Publication

Bahl, Atul, author, editor
    Recognizing an historic injustice : Canada's first national
internment operations, 1914-1920 : a unit of secondary students
exploring the events, causes and consequences : the internment
and suppression of thousands of individuals in Canada during
the First World War era / authors, Atul Bahl, Ilan Danjoux,
Lindsay Gibson, James Miles ; editors, Atul Bahl, Roland Case.

(Pivotal voices)
Includes bibliographical references and index.
ISBN 978-0-86491-372-2 (pbk.)

    1. Ukrainian Canadians--Evacuation and relocation, 1914-1920--
Study and teaching (Secondary)--Canada. 2. World War, 1914-1918--
concentration camps--Study and teaching (Secondary)--Canada.
3. World War, 1914-1918--Study and teaching (Secondary)--Canada.
I. Case, Roland, 1951-, editor II. Danjoux, Ilan, author III. Gibson,
Lindsay, 1975-, author IV. Miles, James, 1984- , author V. Title
VI. Series: Pivotal voices

D627.C2B34 2014   940.3'17710712   C2014-906923-5

Introduction

Critical Challenges

Blackline Masters and Documents

Contents

About the series

Recognizing An Historic Injustice: Canada's First National Internment Operations, 1914-1920 is the second publication in the *Pivotal Voices* series. This series seeks to embed multiple voices in the teaching of history. Since it is impossible and unproductive to try to represent all conceivable perspectives on a given event, we focus on key groups that are likely to differ from one another, and whose stories have not been sufficiently told. The series title—pivotal voices—reflects this approach and our attempts to present various groups' stories in their own words.

About this publication

The objective of this publication is to raise critical awareness among secondary school students about the largely unknown story of Canada's first national internment operations between 1914 and 1920. During this period the federal government interned thousands of Ukrainians, Bulgarians, Croatians, Czechs, Germans, Hungarians, Italians, Jews, various people from the Ottoman Empire, Polish, Romanians, Russians, Serbians, Slovaks, Slovenes, among others of whom most were Ukrainians and most were civilians. While it is impossible to teach all stories and events in our nation's history, the omission until very recently of this incident, has left a gap in our understanding of Canada's history. It was not until 2008 that the Canadian government recognized this legally sanctioned historical injustice. Part of the pledge to redress this wrong is to educate Canadian youth about the First World War internment era. This publication is an attempt to recognize those who suffered from this injustice and, through greater awareness, ensure that similar injustices are less likely to be to be repeated.

The timing of this publication's launch coincides with two significant markers of Canada's first national internment operations:

- the unveiling of a permanent exhibit about Canada's first national internment operations on September 13, 2013 at the site of the Cave and Basin National Historic Site in Banff National Park, Alberta, where Ukrainians and other Europeans branded as "enemy aliens" were interned.
- the one hundred year anniversary of the Great War (August 4, 1914).

Significance of Canada's first national internment operations

Regarded by historians as the "first great wave of immigration" to Canada, roughly 2.5 million newcomers arrived in the new Dominion between 1896 and 1911. A significant proportion of these immigrants were from Eastern Europe, the majority of which were Ukrainians, who were actively recruited by a government in search of labour to feed its growing resource and agricultural sectors. Lured to the Dominion by promises of "free land" and freedom, these newcomers faced many hardships and struggles in what was often an unwelcoming land. However, the outbreak of the First World War profoundly altered the lives of these migrants in ways they could not have imagined when they left their homeland searching for a better life in Canada.

Having emigrated from territories under the control of the Austro-Hungarian Empire, which was one of the British Empire's adversaries during the First World War, Ukrainians and other Europeans came under increasing suspicion. As wartime anxieties fanned the flames of xenophobia, the passage of the *War Measures Act* on August 22, 1914 provided the legal instrument for an Order In Council by the Canadian Government. Approximately 80,000 individuals were required to register as "enemy aliens" and to report to local authorities on a regular basis. While the majority were Ukrainians, other communities included Germans, Poles, Italians, Bulgarians, Croatians, Serbians, Hungarians, Russians, Jews, Slovaks, Slovenes, Czechs, Armenians, Alevi Kurds, Turks and Romanians. From among these groups, 8,579 individuals including as many as 5,000 Ukrainians were interned in camps across Canada. This marked the beginning of a traumatic period in the history of these affected communities, a crippling legacy some have argued remains evident until this day.

Referred to as Canada's first national internment operations, the period between 1914 and 1920 saw families of those labeled "enemy aliens" separated, their property confiscated and sold, and thousands of men consigned to internment camps and years of forced labour in Canada's wilderness. The infrastructure development programs that received 'free' internee labour benefited the Canadian government and the captains of industry to such an extent that the internment continued for two years after the end of the war. Perhaps most disturbing is the fact that this episode in Canadian history has gone largely overlooked by historians.

During the First World War, the Canadian government and its agents systematically carried out internment operations. Also labeled "enemy aliens" during the Second World War, Japanese, Italian and German Canadians suffered a fate similar to that which befell Ukrainians and other Europeans during the First World War period. These examples of legally sanctioned injustice say the civil rights of targeted Canadians denied without just cause, and entire communities subjected to indignity, abuse and untold suffering, not because of anything they had done, but because of where they came from, and who they were. While the internment operations are a relic of the World Wars, remaining vigilant in the defense of civil liberties and human rights, particularly during periods of domestic or international crisis, remains vitally important.

Xenophobia in Canadian history is often exacerbated during periods of war or when social anxieties are heightened by economic and political uncertainty and upheaval. This has resulted in the persecution and unlawful treatment of members of Canadian society who are among the most vulnerable. It has also resulted in the use of the *War Measures Act* during the First and Second World Wars, and in Quebec during the 1970's October Crisis, to strip Canadians of their civil liberties. By critically examining First World War internment, we can help students understand the myriad forces that give rise to legally sanctioned social injustices. It is hoped that such an understanding will reduce the likelihood of future injustices. With this resource, secondary school students will be afforded an opportunity to learn about the past, so that they may be better able to understand their present and actively and constructively plan for a more socially just future.

Considered the last survivor of Canada's First National Internment Operation, Mary (Manko) Haskett's 1993 letter to Prime Minister Brian Mulroney seeking acknowledgement and redress for those who suffered great hardships and loss, sheds light on this tragic chapter in Canadian history.

29 March 1993

I was 6 when I was interned, along with my parents, Andrew and Katherine, my brother John, and my sisters Anne and Carolka. She was only two and a half years old when she died at the Spirit Lake internment camp in Quebec. I may be the last survivor of Canada's first national internment operations. What happened to our family, to many of our friends from Montreal's Ukrainian-Canadian community, and to my sister Carolka, can never be undone. It was unwarranted. It was unjust.

But I believe that you, Mr. Prime Minister, have a unique and historic opportunity to show understanding and compassion for those who fell victim. Before you leave office I appeal to you to honour the Ukrainian Canadian community's request for acknowledgement and redress. *I do this on behalf of my parents, for those many thousands of others who can no longer speak, for my sister Carolka. Our community, all of us, suffered a national humiliation. Few Canadians, even today, realize how traumatic and damaging those internment operations were. My own children did not believe me when I told them I had been interned in Canada.* Spirit Lake is no longer shown in any atlas. Canadian history books do not mention how thousands of Ukrainians were interned, disenfranchised and otherwise mistreated in this country between 1914-1920. Until recently, I did not even know where Carolka was buried. I believe you can appreciate how important it is for me to have this injustice dealt with in my lifetime. I hope you will take my appeal to heart and do what is right and just.

(Signed) Mary (Manko) Haskett

Mary Haskett (Manko), "Internment survivor writes Mulroney" in Lubomyr Luciuk (ed.), *Righting an Injustice* (Toronto, ON: The Justinian Press, 1994), p. 151.

Each **critical challenge** opens with a **question** or **task** which is the focal activity upon which the lesson is based. An **overview** describes the topic and the main activities that students undertake.

Broad understanding is the intended curricular understanding that will emerge as students work through the challenge.

Requisite tools provides an inventory of specific intellectual resources that students need to competently address the critical challenge:

 Background knowledge—the information about the topic required for thoughtful reflection;

 Criteria for judgment—the considerations or grounds for deciding which of the alternatives is the most sensible or appropriate;

 Critical thinking vocabulary—the concepts and distinctions that help students to think critically about the topic;

 Thinking strategies—procedures, organizers, models, or algorithms that help in thinking through the challenge;

 Habits of mind—the values and attitudes of a careful and conscientious thinker that are especially relevant to the critical challenge.

The body of the lesson is found under **suggested activities** that indicate how the critical challenge may be introduced and how the requisite tools may be taught.

Where relevant, **sessions** indicate where each anticipated new lesson would begin and list the blackline masters needed for that session.

Down the left-hand panel is a handy **summary of main tasks** or activities for each session.

Icons along the right-hand side point out where specific tools are addressed.

Also provided in **evaluation** are assessment criteria and procedures, and in **extension** are found suggestions for further exploration or broader application of key ideas.

References cited in the suggested activities or recommended for additional information are often listed.

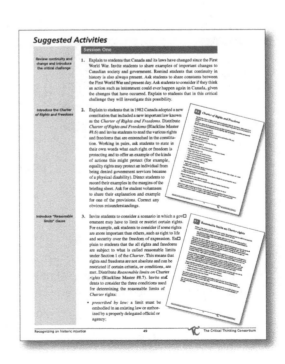

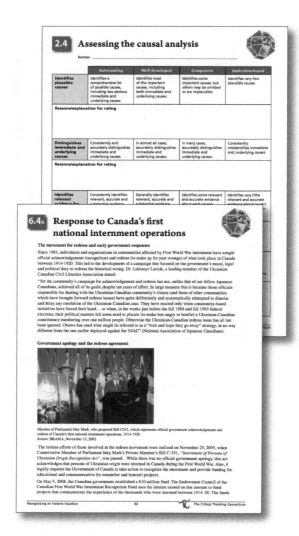

Blackline masters *are found immediately after individual lessons or, in the case of a sequenced unit, at the back of the volume. These are the reproducible learning resources referred to in the suggested activities. They serve a wide range of purposes:*

- **assessment rubrics** *identify suggested criteria and standards for evaluating student work;*

- **briefing sheets** *provide background information for students;*

- **data charts** *contain various organizers for recording and analyzing information;*

- **documents** *refer to primary source material, including paintings and other illustrations;*

- **student activities** *provide questions and tasks for students to complete.*

Electronic resources *supplement to our print publications. These materials include colour reproductions of pictures, primary documents, and updated links to other sites.*

- *If electronic resources had been developed at the time of publication, the available resources are referenced in the list of Resources.*

- *Periodically we update or supplement the print volumes with additional electronic information and resources.*

For more information about our model of critical thinking consult our website — www.tc2.ca.

To locate referenced materials or to see whether new material has been developed, access our website and look for the title of this publication under the the Pivotal Voices *pages: http://tc2.ca/pv.php*

Understanding critical thinking

Critical thinking involves thinking through problematic situations about what to believe or how to act where the thinker makes reasoned judgments that embody the qualities of a competent thinker.

A person is attempting to think critically when she thoughtfully seeks to assess what would be sensible or reasonable to believe or do in a given situation. The need to reach reasoned judgments may arise in countless kinds of problematic situations such as trying to understand a passage in a text, trying to improve an artistic performance, making effective use of a piece of equipment, or deciding how to act in a delicate social situation. What makes these situations problematic is that there is some doubt as to the most appropriate option.

Critical thinking is sometimes contrasted with problem solving, decision making, analysis and inquiry. We see these latter terms for rational deliberation as occasions for critical thinking. In all these situations, we need to think critically about the available options. There is limited value in reaching solutions or making choices that are not sensible or reasonable. Thus, the term critical thinking draws attention to the quality of thinking required to pose and solve problems competently, reach sound decisions, analyze issues, plan and conduct thoughtful inquiries and so on. In other words, thinking critically is a way of carrying out these thinking tasks just as being careful is a way of walking down the stairs. Thus, thinking critically is not a unique *type* of thinking that is different from other types of thinking; rather, it refers to the *quality* of thinking. The association of critical thinking with being negative or judgmental is misleading, since the reference to critical is to distinguish it from uncritical thinking—thinking that accepts conclusions at face value without any assessment of their merits or bases. It is more fruitful to interpret critical in the sense of critique—looking at the merits and shortcomings of alternatives in order to arrive at a reasoned judgment.

Our focus on the quality of thinking does not imply that students must arrive at a preconceived right answer; rather, we look to see whether their varied responses exhibit the qualities that characterize good thinking in a given situation. For example, it wouldn't matter whether students opposed or supported a position expressed in a newspaper or textbook. Regardless of their particular position, we would want students' critically thoughtful responses to exhibit sensitivity to any bias, consider alternative points of view, attend to the clarity of key concepts, and assess supporting evidence. We believe that emphasis on qualities that student responses should exhibit focusses teachers' attention on the crucial dimension in promoting and assessing students' competence in thinking critically. The challenge for teachers is to adopt practices that will effectively promote these qualities in their students.

Promoting critical thinking

To help students improve as critical thinkers, we propose a four-pronged approach:

- build a *community of thinkers* within the school and classroom;
- infuse opportunities for critical thinking—what we call *critical challenges*—throughout the curriculum;
- develop the *intellectual tools* that will enable students to become competent critical thinkers;
- on a continuing basis, *assess students' competence* in using the intellectual tools to think through critical challenges.

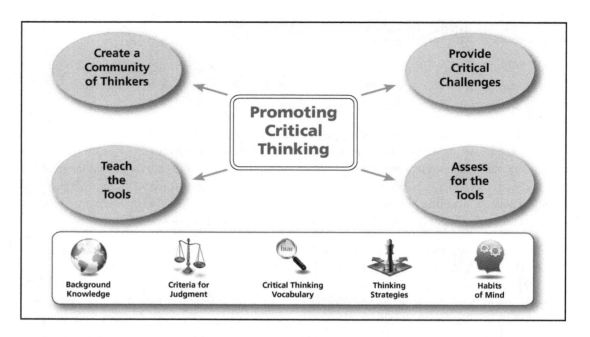

Building a community of thinkers

Developing supportive school and classroom communities where reflective inquiry is valued may be the most important factor in nurturing critical thinking. Many of the intellectual resources, the "tools" of critical thinking, will not be mastered by students unless their use is reinforced on an ongoing basis. As well, the image of the thinker as a solitary figure is misleading. No one person can perfectly embody all the desired attributes—we must learn to rely on others to complement our own thoughts. There are many routines and norms that teachers can adopt to create a community of thinkers:

- Regularly pose questions and assignments requiring students to think through, and not merely recall, what is being learned.

- Create ongoing opportunities to engage in critical and cooperative dialogue—confer, inquire, debate, and critique—is key to creating a community of thinkers.

- Employ self- and peer-evaluation as ways of involving students in thinking critically about their own work.

- Model good critical thinking practices. Students are more likely to learn to act in desired ways if they see teachers making every effort to be open-minded, to seek clarification where needed, to avoid reaching conclusions based on inadequate evidence, and so on.

Infusing critical challenges throughout the curriculum

If students are to improve their ability to think critically, they must have numerous opportunities to engage with and think through problematic situations—what we refer to as *critical challenges*.

- *Does the question or task require judgment?* A question or task is a critical challenge only if it invites students to assess the reasonableness of plausible options or alternative conclusions. In short, it must require more than retrieval of information, rote application of a strategy, uninformed guessing, or mere assertion of a preference.

- *Will the challenge be meaningful to students?* Trivial, decontextualized mental exercises often alienate or bore students. It is important to frame challenges that are likely to engage students in tackling questions and tasks that they will find meaningful.

- *Does the challenge address key aspects of the subject matter?* Critical thinking should not be divorced from the rest of the curriculum. Students are more likely to learn the content of the curriculum if they are invited to think critically about issues embedded in the subject matter.

- *Do students have the tools or can they reasonably acquire the tools needed to competently address the challenge?* Students need support in acquiring the essential tools required to competently meet the critical challenge.

Developing intellectual tools for thinking critically

The key to helping students develop as critical thinkers is to nurture competent use of five types of tools of thinking. These categories of tools are *background knowledge*, *criteria for judgment*, *critical thinking vocabulary*, *thinking strategies*, and *habits of mind*.

	Background Knowledge —*the information about a topic required for thoughtful reflection*	Students cannot think deeply about a topic if they know little about it. Two questions to ask in developing this tool: • What background information do students need for them to make a well-informed judgment on the matter before them? • How can students be assisted in acquiring this information in a meaningful manner?
	Criteria for Judgment —*the considerations or grounds for deciding which of the alternatives is the most sensible or appropriate*	Critical thinking is essentially a matter of judging which alternative is sensible or reasonable. Students need help in thinking carefully about the criteria to use when judging various alternatives: • Is my estimate *accurate*? • Is the interpretation *plausible*? • Is the conclusion *fair* to all? • Is my proposal *feasible*?
	Critical Thinking Vocabulary —*the range of concepts and distinctions that are helpful when thinking critically*	Students require the vocabulary or concepts that permit them to make important distinctions among the different issues and thinking tasks facing them. These include the following: • inference and direct observation; • generalization and over-generalization; • premise and conclusion; • bias and point of view.
	Thinking Strategies —*the repertoire of heuristics, organizing devices, models and algorithms that may be useful when thinking through a critical thinking problem*	Although critical thinking is never simply a matter of following certain procedures or steps, numerous strategies are useful for guiding one's performance when thinking critically: • *Making decisions:* Are there models or procedures to guide students through the factors they should consider (e.g., a framework for issue analysis or problem solving)? • *Organizing information:* Would a graphic organizer (e.g., webbing diagrams, Venn diagrams, "pro and con" charts) be useful in representing what a student knows about an issue? • *Role taking:* Before deciding on an action that affects others, should students put themselves in the others' positions and imagine their feelings?
	Habits of Mind —*the values and attitudes of a careful and conscientious thinker*	Being able to apply criteria and use strategies is of little value unless students also have the habits of mind of a thoughtful person. These include being: • *Open-minded:* Are students willing to consider evidence opposing their view and to revise their view if the evidence warrants it? • *Fair-minded:* Are students willing to give impartial consideration to alternative points of view and not simply to impose their preference? • *Independent-minded:* Are students willing to stand up for their firmly held beliefs? • *Inquiring or "critical" attitude:* Are students inclined to question the clarity of and support for claims and to seek justified beliefs and values?

Assessing for the tools

Assessment is an important complement to teaching the tools of critical thinking. As suggested by the familiar adages "What is counted counts" and "Testing drives the curriculum," evaluation has important implications for what students consider important and ultimately what students learn. Evaluations that focus exclusively on recall of information or never consider habits of mind fail to assess, and possibly discourage, student growth in critical reflection.

A key challenge in assessing critical thinking is deciding what to look for in a student's answer. If there is no single correct response, we may well ask: "On what basis, then, can we reliably assess students?" In the case of critical thinking, we would want to see how well students exhibited the qualities of a competent thinker. Thus, the intellectual resources or tools for critical thinking become the criteria for assessing students' work. The following example suggests specific assessment criteria for each of the five types of critical thinking tools that might be considered when evaluating critical thinking in an argumentative essay and an artistic work.

Type of criteria for assessment	Evidence of critical thinking in a persuasive essay	Evidence of critical thinking in an artistic work
Background Knowledge *Has the student provided adequate and accurate information?*	• cited accurate information.	• revealed knowledge of the mechanics of the medium.
Criteria for Judgment *Has the student satisfied relevant criteria for judgment?*	• provided ample evidence; • arranged arguments in logical sequence.	• was imaginative; • was clear and forceful.
Critical Thinking Vocabulary *Has the student revealed understanding of important vocabulary?*	• correctly distinguished arguments from counter-arguments.	• represented point of view.
Thinking Strategies *Has the student made effective use of appropriate thinking strategies?*	• used appropriate strategies for persuasive writing.	• employed suitable rehearsal/ preparation strategies.
Habits of Mind *Has the student demonstrated the desired habits of mind?*	• demonstrated an openness to alternative perspectives; • refrained from forming firm opinions where the evidence was inconclusive.	• was open to constructive criticism; • demonstrated a commitment to high quality; • demonstrated a willingness to take risks with the medium.

The lesson plans in this collection are self-contained. Each provides detailed instructional strategies and the required support materials including excerpts from primary and secondary sources for student use. These include briefing sheets and activity sheets (Blackline Masters) that are printed at the back of this book, and source documents and videos that are linked to readily accessible websites.

Many of the lessons can be taught on a stand-alone basis. If taught individually, these lessons are ideally suited for Canadian History courses, as well as the study of legally sanctioned injustices in courses such as Civics, Law and Politics. As components of a unit of study, these lessons invite critical inquiry into a wide range of topics and issues relating to the impact of First World War internment operations on affected communities in Canada.

1	**Should this event be in the curriculum?** 2 sessions	In this introductory challenge, students consider whether Canada's first national internment operations during the WWI era ought to be a topic of study in the curriculum. Students begin by identifying significant or important events in their own lives. They consider events that varying in their level of significance, ranging for globally or nationally significant to merely personal importance or complete insignificance. Students then read accounts of internments in Canada during the WWI and WWII eras, and consider why one is typically included in the curriculum and the other is rarely profiled. They then rate the historical significance of First World War internment operations deciding at what level this topic should be included in the curriculum.
2	**Why did it happen?** 2 sessions	In this two-part challenge, students learn to identify the range of underlying and immediate causes leading to Canada's first national internment operations during the World War I era. Students are first introduced to the concept of causation by identifying various factors that contributed to a fictional car accident. They learn to distinguish between underlying and immediate causes. Students then consider criteria for assessing the importance of causes. Next students examine various primary and secondary sources to gather information about the contributing role of various factors to World War I internment. They identify the many underlying or immediate causal factors that contributed to the decision to intern "enemy aliens" and gather evidence about their impact. Finally, students determine the three most important contributing factors to the event.
3	**What were the camps like?** 3 sessions	In this three-part critical challenge, students learn about the experiences of those who were interned during the World War I era. Students are introduced to the idea of historical perspective-taking using an example of postal services in the nineteenth century. They consider the difference between presentism and historical perspective-taking and learn about three strategies to help in adopting a historical perspective. Students then examine various primary and secondary sources to learn about life in the internment camps from an internee's perspective. They record relevant details from the sources, draw possible conclusions and summarize what they have learned about internee's experiences. Drawing upon these findings, students write a letter from the point of view of a teenager at the time explaining the experience.
4	**What was the impact of internment on individuals?** 2 sessions	In this two-part challenge, students identify and assess the direct and indirect consequences of internment on Ukrainians and others in Canada. Students learn to recognize when something is the consequence of a prior event, and to distinguish consequences that follow directly from an event from those that are indirect. Students create a web of effects to illustrate the direct and indirect consequences resulting from an event in their own lives. They then turn their attention to the consequences of Canada's first national internment operations. Using various sources, students identify the various direct and indirect consequences of World War I internment, and classify the consequences into four categories: psychological/emotional, social/cultural, economic and political/legal. Finally, students rate the severity of the impact of each category of consequence.
5	**How did internment change the communities?** 3 sessions	In this two-part challenge, students investigate the continuities and changes in conditions experienced by members of the affected communities before and after World War I. Students begin by tracking similarities and differences at two comparison points in their own lives: primary school and secondary school. After discussing criteria that can be used to assess their relative importance, students identify the most important similarity and most important difference between these two periods in their lives. Students work in groups to analyze primary and secondary sources to obtain information about the political, social and economic conditions experienced by Ukrainian Canadians before and after World War I internment. They identify a range of similarities and differences and identify the most important of these in the pre- and post-war periods.

6 **How adequately has the government responded?**

2 sessions

In this challenge, students consider the adequacy of official government responses to several of Canada's legally sanctioned injustices, including the first national internment operations. To begin, students explore a contemporary school-related scenario to learn about criteria that can be used to judge the adequacy of a response to a legally-sanctioned but unjust act. Working in groups, students examine official government responses to one of four historic injustices in Canada (the internment of Japanese Canadians in World War II, Residential Schools that Canada's indigenous peoples were forced to attend, the Head Tax imposed on Chinese immigrants, the refusal to allow the passengers of the *Komogata Maru* to disembark in Canada). Students compare the arguments for and against the adequacy of the official response to their assigned incident and share their findings with rest of the class. Student rank-order these four responses in terms of their adequacy. Next, students turn their attention to the government's response to the unjust treatment of vRious ethnic communities during the World War I era. They rate each element of the response (apology, if applicable, and redress, agreement/compensation). Students communicate their conclusions with possible improvements in a letter to a government official.

7 **What should we all know?**

1 session

Students decide what are the most important features of Canada's First World War internment operations. Students review the key details of the event. They then think of four aspects that might be worth remembering about an injustice: what went on (key events), why it happened (causes), what happened as a result (consequences) and what might we learn from the event (lessons learned). Students apply these questions to a video of an interview about the interment operations on the regional and national dimensions of the event prior to compiling the information they have learned in this unit. When students have pulled together their information on the four aspects from previous lessons in the unit, they decide upon eight features of First World War internment that most need to be captured in their educational campaign. As a concluding activity, they share their findings with their group members and try to agree collectively on the key ideas for each of the four aspects of the injustice.

8 **Could it happen again?**

3 sessions

In this two-part challenge, students determine how the First World War internment operation may have been different had the *Charter of Rights and Freedoms* been in place and whether such a scenario could happen again. Students consider what government actions during internment would have been infractions or violations under the *Charter of Rights and Freedoms*, if it had been in effect at the time. Students apply the *Reasonable Limits* conditions under Section 1 of the *Charter* to determine the constitutionality of each government action. Students consider both the context of the time and the *War Measures Act*. In the second part of the challenge, students turn their attention to the restrictions or additional protections a present-day government of today would have to provide before it could invoke a law similar to the *War Measures Act*. Finally, students decide whether a similar situation could happen again considering the contemporary context and current legislation.

9 **How can we educate others?**

2 sessions

In this two-part challenge, students learn how they might educate Canadians about World War I internment in Canada. They begin by considering the purpose and function of commemorative displays or memorials. They develop criteria for creating a powerful commemorative, and apply these to examples from around the world. After hearing other students' critiques, each student chooses the two most powerful commemoratives. In the second part of the challenge, students design the format for a commemorative display they will create to educate Canadians about the causes, key events, consequences and lessons learned from World War I internment that they identified in Lesson 7. Students complete an initial design, receive peer feedback and refine their design. Students exhibit their completed commemorative displays for others in their school or community, explaining the selections they have made and the importance of remembering World War I internment. Finally, students write a brief reflection on what they have learned through this unit about the importance of recognizing those who have suffered past injustices.

The following books, films and other resources may be useful to teachers and students in learning more about the issues and topics addressed in this publication.

Texts

D H Avery, *'Dangerous Foreigners': European Immigrant Workers and Labour Radicalism in Canada 1896-1932* (Toronto: McClelland and Stewart, 1979)

___, *Reluctant Host: Canada's Response to Immigrant Workers, 1896 – 1994* (Toronto: McClelland & Stewart, 1995)

D J Carter, *POW – Behind Canadian Barbed Wire: Alien, Refugee and Prisoner of War Camps in Canada 1914-1946* (rev 2nd edition, Calgary: Eagle Butte Press, 1998)

J Farney and B S Kordan, "Predicament of Belonging: The Status of Enemy Aliens in Canada, 1914: *Journal of Canadian Studies*, Winter, 2005

J B Gregorovich, ed, *Ukrainian Canadians in Canada's Wars: Materials for Ukrainian Canadian History* (Toronto: Ukrainian Canadian Research Foundation, 1987)

___, ed, *Commemorating An Injustice: Fort Henry and Ukrainian Canadians as "enemy aliens" during the First World War* (Kingston: Kashtan Press, 1994)

B S Kordan, *Enemy Aliens, Prisoners of War: Internment in Canada During the Great War* (Montreal & Kingston: McGill-Queen's University Press, 2002)

B S Kordan and C Mahovsky, *A Bare and Impolitic Right: Internment and Ukrainian-Canadian Redress* (Montreal & Kingston: McGill-Queen's University Press, 2004)

B S Kordan and P Melnycky, *In the Shadow of the Rockies: Diary of the Castle Mountain Internment Camp, 1915-1917* (Edmonton: Canadian Institute of Ukrainian Studies Press, 1991)

L Y Luciuk, *Internment Operations: The Role of Old Fort Henry in World War 1* (Kingston: Delta, 1980)

___, ed, *Righting An Injustice: The Debate Over Redress for Canada's First National Internment Operations* (Toronto: Justinian Press, 1994)

___, *Searching for Place: Ukrainian Displaced Persons, Canada and the Migration of Memory* (Toronto: University of Toronto Press, 2nd rev ed, 2001)

___, *In Fear of the Barbed Wire Fence: Canada's First National Internment Operations and the Ukrainian Canadians, 1914-1920* (Kingston: Kashtan Press, 2001)

L Y Luciuk, *Without Just Cause: Canada's First World War Internment Operations, 1914-1920* (Kingston: Kashtan Press, 2006)

L Y Luciuk and B S Kordan, *Creating A Landscape: A Geography of Ukrainians in Canada* (Toronto: University of Toronto Press, 1989)

L Y Luciuk and Ron Sorobey, *Konowal: A Canadian Hero* (Kingston: Kashtan Press, 2000)

L Y Luciuk and B Sydoruk, *"In My Charge" – The Canadian Internment Camp Photographs of Sergeant William Buck* (Kingston: Kashtan Press, 1997)

L Y Luciuk with N Yurieva and R Zakaluzny, comps, *Roll Call: Lest We Forget* (Kingston: Kashtan Press, 1999)

O Martynowych, *Ukrainians in Canada: The Formative Years, 1891-1924* (Edmonton: Canadian Institute of Ukrainian Studies Press, 1991)

P Melnycky, "Badly Treated in Every Way: The Internment of Ukrainians in Quebec During the First World War," in A Biega and M Diakowsky, eds, *The Ukrainian Experience in Quebec* (Toronto: Basilian Press, 1994)

M Minenko, "Without Just Cause: Canada's First National Internment Operations," in L Luciuk & S Hryniuk, eds, *Canada's Ukrainians: Negotiating An Identity* (Toronto: University of Toronto Press, 1991)

P Peppin, "Emergency Legislation and Rights in Canada: The War Measures Act and Civil Liberties," *Queen's Law Journal*, Kingston: Faculty of Law, Volume 18, 1, 1993

J Petryshyn, *Peasants in the Promised Land: Canada and the Ukrainians, 1891-1914* Toronto: James Lorimer Company, 1985)

A Sendzikas, *Stanley Barracks: Toronto's Military Legacy* (Toronto: Natural Heritage Books, 2011)

F Swyripa and J H Thompson, eds, *Loyalties in Conflict: Ukrainians in Canada During the Great War* (Edmonton: Canadian Institute of Ukrainian Studies, 1982)

J H Thompson, *The Harvest of War: The Prairie West, 1914-1918* (Toronto: McClelland and Stewart, 1978)

B Waiser, *Park Prisoners: The Untold Story of Canada's National Parks, 1915-1946* (Saskatoon: Firth House, 1995)

Films

Unspoken Territory by Marusya Bociurkiw (Moving Images, 2000) www.marusya.ca

La Fuite by Robert Cornellier (1995) www.macumbainternational.com

Freedom Had A Price: Canada's First National Internment Operation by Yurij Luhovy, (National Film Board of Canada, 1994) www.yluhovy.com

Jajo's Secret by James Motluk (Guerrilla Films, 2009) www.guerrillafilms.com

Music

Donna Creighton, *"Look! Eighty Thousand Voices"* 2004, (Hania Metulynsky, bandura), Shipwreckerds Production www.donnacreighton.com

Maria Dunn, *"In The Shadow of the Rockies/As I Walk Through Canada,"* (Brian Cherwick, tsymbaly), 2004 (on the CD "We Were Good People," Distant Whisper Music), Website: www.mariadunn.com

Children's & Young Adult Literature/Plays

Karen Autio, *Sabotage* (Winlaw, British Columbia: Sononis Press, 2013) http://www.karenautio.com/Sabotage.html

Sylvie Brien, *Spirit Lake* (Montreal: Gallimard (ÉDITIONS), 2008) http://www.sylviebrien.com/roman_jeunesse.php?ID=50

Dan Ebbs, *Home and Native Land* (Woodstock, Ontario: Cardinal House, 2005)

Robert Fothergill, *Detaining Mr. Trotsky* (Toronto: Playwrights Guild of Canada, 1987)

Laura Langston, *Lesia's Dream* (Toronto: Harper Collins, 2003) http://www.lauralangston.com/

Barbara Sapergia, *Blood and Salt* (Regina: Coteau Books, 2012) http://coteaubooks.com/

Danny Schur, *Strike! The Musical* (Winnipeg: Strike! Musical Limited Patrtnership, 2005) www.strikemusical.com

Marsha Forchuk Skrypuch, *Silver Threads* (Toronto: Fitzhenry & Whiteside, 2004) with illustrations by M Martchenko www.calla2.com

Marsha Forchuk Skrypuch, *Dear Canada, Prisoners in the Promised Land.* (Markham: Scholastic Canada, 2007) www.calla2.com

Teachers' Guides

Don Quinlan, ed, "Enemy Aliens," *World Affairs Defining Canada's Role* (Toronto: Oxford University Press, 1998)

Social Program Educational Group, Queen's University, "Ukrainian Canadians, "World War I, Canadians in the Global Community: *War, Peace and Security* (CRB Heritage Project: Toronto, Prentice Hall Ginn, 1997)

Douglas Davis, *Prisoners of Prejudice: Canada's first national internment operations, 1914-1920.* (Edmonton Public Schools, 2011)

Credit: This bibliography was prepared by Canada's First World War Internment Recognition Fund, and is reprinted with permission.

Should this event be in the curriculum?

Critical Challenge

Critical task　　Rate the significance of Canada's first national internment operations as a topic of study in the curriculum.

Overview　　In this introductory challenge, students consider whether Canada's first national internment operations during the World War I era ought to be a topic of study in the curriculum. Students begin by identifying significant or important events in their own lives. They consider events that vary in significance from those with global or national significance to those of personal importance or complete insignificance. Students then read accounts of internments that occurred in Canada during the World War I and World War II eras, and consider why one is typically included in the curriculum and the other is rarely profiled. They then rate the historical significance of World War I internment and decide at what level this topic should be included in the curriculum.

Objectives

Broad understanding　　Knowledge that what is included or excluded in history textbooks represents a judgment that people make about the historical significance of an event.

Requisite tools

Background knowledge
- knowledge of the internment of European Canadians during World War I, and of Japanese Canadians during World War II
- knowledge of what historical events are significant, and how educational materials are selected for inclusion in the curriculum

Criteria for judgment
- criteria for judging historical significance based on:
  - the importance and duration of an event at the time
  - the profound and widespread consequences of the event
  - the symbolic or continuing legacy of the event

Critical thinking vocabulary
- historical significance

Thinking strategies
- comparison chart
- rating scale

Required Resources

Activity sheets
Comparing events   Blackline Master #1.2

Briefing sheets
Internment in Canada   Blackline Master #1.1
Background on Canada's
   first national internment   Blackline Master #1.3
Rating historical significance   Blackline Master #1.4

Videos
Historical significance
TC² website (Thinking about history: Video resources): http://tc2.ca/
   teaching-resources/special-collections/thinking-about-history.php

Assessment rubrics
Assessing the rating
   of historical significance   Blackline Master #1.5

The communities affected by the internment operations include Ukrainians, Bulgarians, Croatians, Czechs, Germans, Hungarians, Italians, Jews, various people from the Ottoman Empire, Polish, Romanians, Russians, Serbians, Slovaks, Slovenes, among others of which most were Ukrainians and most were civilians.

Suggested Activities

Provide a personal context for the lesson

1. Begin by asking students to consider the significant events in their personal lives. Invite them to make a list in their notebooks of five or six important personal events. Discuss with students how they decided which events to include (for example, it had a big impact on me; it changed things; looking back, it was a turning point). Point out to students that lots of events have happened in their lives, but that they do not consider all events to be of equal importance. Ask students:

   • Should the personal events they listed in their notebooks be included in the textbook for this course?

   • Why are some events included in a textbook and others are not?

Introduce levels of historical significance

2. Explain to students that what is considered educationally and historically important and therefore deemed worthy of studying in school is a judgment made by education officials, historians, textbook writers, teachers and students. Invite students to think of one event for each of the following categories:

   • globally significant: every student in the world should study this event

   • nationally significant: every student in the country where it occurred should study it

   • regionally significant: every student in the region where it occurred or who belongs to the specific group(s) affected should study it

   • individually significant: the descendants and family of the people involved should study it

   • not at all significant: not worth remembering.

Compare two historical events

3. Without revealing the identity of the events described (internment during World War I of European Canadians and internment during World War II of Japanese Canadians), ask students to compare the significance of two historical events that occurred in Canada. Distribute the background information sheet, *Internment in Canada* (Blackline Master #1.1), and the activity sheet, *Comparing events* (Blackline Master #1.2), to each student (or pair of students). Direct them to read the two accounts and record important information about each internment. Once this is completed, ask them to assess the relative significance of each event and make note of reasons for their decision.

4. Invite students to share their conclusions about the significance of the two events. Focus the discussion on the factors or criteria used to evaluate historical significance. Drawing on student comments, formulate three criteria:

- importance and duration of the event at the time

- the profound and widespread consequences of the event

- the symbolic or continuing legacy of the event

5. Point out to students that the two accounts they read both describe the internment of civilians in Canada, once during World War I and a second time during World War II. Based on the reading, ask students to summarize their understanding of internment and internment camps. Ask students whether they know which groups of Canadian civilians were interned during these wars. If students are unfamiliar with the internment of Ukrainians and other Europeans during World War I and Japanese Canadians during World War II, ask students why such important events in Canadian history are not widely known? Inform students that although World War II internment is widely covered in textbooks and taught in secondary schools, World War I internment is not. Ask students why they think this may be the case.

Session Two

1. Before students assess the significance of World War I internment, arrange for them to view *Historical Significance*, a short video on The Critical Thinking Consortium website, and to read the briefing sheet, *Background on Canada's first national internment operations* (Blackline Master #1.3). These sources offer additional information about the event and its consequences. Encourage students to makes notes on any information they find in these sources that relate to the three criteria for historical significance discussed earlier.

Offer a rating of significance

2. Distribute a copy of activity sheet, *Rating historical significance* (Blackline Master #1.4) to each student. Using evidence from the video, the written description of Event 1 and the background sheet, invite students to rate the historical significance of World War I internment in light of each of the three criteria listed. They should then offer an overall assessment, deciding at what level this topic should be included in the curriculum.

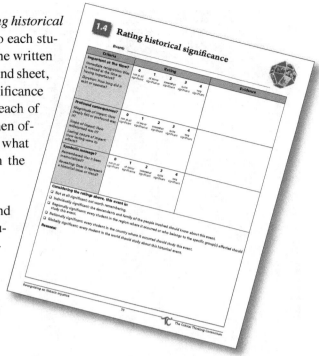

Share judgments

3. Ask students, first in small groups and later as a class, to discuss their conclusions, focussing on the reasons presented rather than seeking agreement among students.

Evaluation

1. Use the rubric on *Assessing the rating of historical significance* (Blackline Master #1.5) to assess the conclusions students recorded on Blackline Master #1.4.

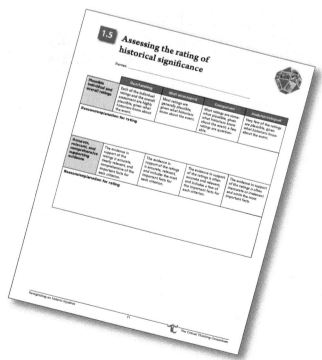

Castle Mountain statue "Why" by John Boxtel.

Why did it happen?

Critical Challenge

Critical tasks

A. Identify the various underlying and immediate causes of World War I era internment.

B. Determine the three most important contributing factors to World War I era internment.

Overview

In this two-part challenge, students learn to identify the range of underlying and immediate causes leading to Canada's first national internment operations between 1914–1920. Students are first introduced to the concept of causation by identifying various factors that contributed to a fictional car accident. They learn to distinguish between underlying and immediate causes. Students then consider criteria for assessing the importance of causes. Next students examine various primary and secondary sources to gather information about the contributing role of various factors to World War I internment. They identify the many underlying or immediate causal factors that contributed to the decision to intern "enemy aliens" and gather evidence about their impact. Finally, students determine the three most important contributing factors to the event.

Objectives

Broad understanding

Legally sanctioned social injustices are complex historical events that have immediate and underlying causes.

Requisite tools

Background knowledge
- knowledge of the immediate and underlying causes of Canada's first national internment operations

Criteria for judgment
- criteria for determining causal importance, including:
  - causal factor is directly linked to the event occurring
  - causal factors are important contributors to the direction and intensity of an event
  - the event would be much less likely to have occurred if the factor was not present

Critical thinking vocabulary
- causation

Thinking strategies

 The Critical Thinking Consortium

Habits of mind
- attention to detail

Required Resources

Source documents

Reasons for World War I internment

TC² website (History Docs): http://sourcedocs.tc2.ca/history-docs/
   topics/world-war-i-internment/reasons-for-ww-i-internment.html

Primary source #1 The War Measures Act

Primary source #2: Report on Iwan Milan

Primary source #6: Arrest of Ukrainian socialists

Primary source #7: Enemy aliens

Secondary source #1: Motivations and justifications for internment

Secondary source #2 Economic misfortune

Secondary source #3: Divided loyalties

Activity sheets

Identifying the causes of the accident	Blackline Master #2.1
Sorting immediate and underlying causes	Blackline Master #2.2
Examining causal factors	Blackline Master #2.3

Briefing sheets

Background on Canada's first national internment operations	Blackline Master #1.3

Videos

Historical significance

TC² website (Thinking about history: Video resources): http://tc2.ca/
   teaching-resources/special-collections/thinking-about-history.php

Internee descendants

Canadian First World War Internment Recognition Fund website
   (YouTube video series): http://www.internmentcanada.ca/pop-
   video4.html

Cause and consequence

TC² website (Thinking about History: Video resources) http://tc2.ca/
   teaching-resources/special-collections/thinking-about-history.php

Assessment rubrics

Assessing the causal analysis	Blackline Master #2.4

The communities affected by the internment operations include Ukrainians, Bulgarians, Croatians, Czechs, Germans, Hungarians, Italians, Jews, various people from the Ottoman Empire, Polish, Romanians, Russians, Serbians, Slovaks, Slovenes, among others of which most were Ukrainians and most were civilians.

Suggested Activities

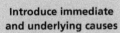

Introduce the concept of causation

1. Explain to students that when historians study the past, they do more than simply recount a sequence of events. They strive to explain why events happened the way they did. Historians often ask questions such as, "What caused World War I?" or "Did increased use of birth control affect women's status in society?" In asking these questions, historians are not looking for a single factor that caused the event; rather, they are trying to identify the many factors, including broad social, political and economic conditions, that contributed to its occurrence.

Recognize various causal factors

2. Invite students to identify a range of causes by considering a series of events leading to a fictional car accident. Distribute *Identifying the causes of the accident* (Blackline Master #2.1) to each pair of students and ask them to identify all the possible causes that they can locate in the account of the accident. Invite students to share their lists of contributing factors with the rest of the class.

> **2.1 Identifying the causes of the accident**
>
> Just before midnight one dark and stormy night, a man called John Smith, who worked as an engine mechanic, was sitting in an isolated cabin in the woods. As he reached for a cigarette, he noticed he had only one left. Glancing at his watch, he realized that he had just enough time to hop in his car and drive to the gas station down the road to buy cigarettes before it closed. As he pulled out of his lane onto the highway, his car was soon enough on the highway, his car was hit by his neighbour, who, running from a long night of drinking, was unable to stop his car soon enough on the icy road. Smith was killed instantly. Later, as the townspeople were discussing the sad event, they shook their heads one after another and said, "We always knew that smoking would kill Smith." It is worth noting that local officials had long been warned of the dangers on that part of the highway, especially in winter, and yet they seemed uninterested in doing anything about it. Apparently this was because the residents of that part of the town did not have any influence with local authorities. Others wondered whether, if the impaired driving laws had been more faithfully enforced in the town, whether the neighbour who smashed into Smith would have been as drunk as he was.
>
> List the contributing factors to the accident
>
> [blank box]
>
> Taken from *Heaven & Hell on Earth: The Massacre of the "Black" Donnellys*, part of the Great Unsolved Mysteries in Canadian History series. online: www.canadianmysteries.ca.
>
> Recognizing an historic injustice 72
>
> The Critical Thinking Consortium

Introduce immediate and underlying causes

3. Explain to students that the difficulty in determining causation is that direct causes seldom act on their own as catalysts for change. Often, underlying causes and broader trends create the conditions that trigger significant change. For example, the start of World War I is often attributed to the assassination of Archduke Franz Ferdinand. However, a war does not break out each time a leader is killed. A broader set of circumstances existed that enabled the killing of this leader to trigger a global conflict. These broader factors and circumstances—called underlying causes—are often distinguished from immediate causes:

   - *immediate causes:* the direct and often the most obvious and easily identified factors. They typically occur just prior to the event in question. Removal of immediate causes may not have prevented the occurrence of the event, as there may have been more significant factors contributing to the event.

   - *underlying causes:* the broader and usually less obvious and more difficult to identify conditions. They often represent a broader underlying factor, practice, or belief and are not tied to a single event. Removal of an underlying cause may help prevent the event from occurring.

Introduce the metaphor
of catalyst and
material causes

4. Immediate causes are igniters of events. They are the flints, matches, or lighters that start a fire. An example is Archduke Franz Ferdinand's assassination in the case of World War I. However, if a match, flint, or lighter has no kindling, dry grass or wood to burn, it will quickly fizzle out and will not cause the fire to start. The kindling, dry grass and wood represents the underlying causes that are often the foundational causes of an event, and the causes that propel an event forward. Underlying causes merit attention because they create the circumstances for historical change. In the case of World War I, long-standing national and imperial rivalries among countries in Europe led to an arms race and the formation of alliances long before the archduke's assassination occurred in 1914.

5. Distribute copies of *Sorting immediate and underlying causes* (Blackline Master #2.2) to each pair of students. It lists eight contributing factors to the previously-discussed car accident. Invite students to classify the causes as immediate or underlying. Provide an example of an immediate cause (for example, the victim had run out of cigarettes) and a broader underlying cause (such as the lax law enforcement regarding drunk drivers). After completing the task, invite students to discuss their conclusions. Below are samples of the answers that students might offer.

Immediate causes	Underlying causes
It was late in the evening on a dark and stormy night.	*This part of the highway had long been dangerous and, despite warnings, the authorities had failed to do anything about it.*
Perhaps because he was in a rush, John Smith didn't exercise enough caution when pulling out onto the highway.	*The town council was biased against recommendations and complaints made by people in that part of town.*
The roads were icy and difficult to drive on.	*The neighbour who crashed into John Smith failed to consider the icy conditions on the road.*
The neighbour who crashed into John Smith was driving while impaired from alcohol.	*Liquor laws in the town were not faithfully enforced by the police.*

6. Ask students to consider whether all the causes are equally important—whether some factors are more instrumental than others in bringing about and shaping an event. Distribute copies of *Examining causal factors* (Blackline Master #2.3) to each pair of students.

7. Invite students to consider three criteria for evaluating the importance of causes.

   • The factor was **directly linked** to the event occurring (that is, it gave rise to causes that were catalysts related to the event) and was not simply an accidental occurrence (for example, the fact that the man was a smoker is linked to the accident because the reason he was driving at the time was to purchase cigarettes).

   • The factor was an **important contributor to the direction and intensity** of the event (for example, a careful driver going slowly might still have hit Smith's car but not necessarily killed him).

   • The event **would be much less likely to have occurred if the factor was not present** (that is, Smith may not have been killed that night, but speeding cars may eventually have claimed his life if the highway was dangerous).

8. Ask students to record comments on Blackline Master #2.3 for each of the suggested causes of the accident in light of these three criteria. Once they have done this, invite students to judge the three most important causes that led to the accident. These will be the causes that most fulfill each of the criteria. Arrange for students to share their priority causes and supporting reasons. As a class, attempt to reach consensus on the most important causes for the accident.

9. OPTIONAL: For further explanation of historical causation, invite students to watch the short video, *Cause and consequence*, found on The Critical Thinking Consortium website. Discuss the examples and the factors explained in this video.

Provide historical context to World War I internment

1. Inform students that they will now consider the factors that contributed to the Canadian government decision to intern civilians during World War I. If students did not complete Challenge #1: Should this event be in the curriculum?, provide some historical context for this event. You may wish to review what students already know, and then assign one or more of the following activities:

   • View two short videos on the World War I internment: *Historical significance*, on The Critical Thinking Consortium website, and *Internee descendants*, on the Canadian First World War Internment Recognition Fund website.

   • Read the briefing sheet, *Background on Canada's first national internment operations* (Blackline Master #1.3).

Introduce the critical task

2. Inform students that they will now examine various primary and secondary sources in order to determine the immediate and underlying causes of Canada's first national internment operations. They will identify possible factors, look for evidence demonstrating the influence of each factor on the event and then judge the three most important causes of this historical injustice.

Model the analysis

3. Distribute a copy of the organizer, *Examining causal factors* (Blackline Master #2.3) and a copy of *History Doc #1: The War Measures Act* (found on The Critical Thinking Consortium website) to each student. As a class, read the document and pause to discuss important/difficult concepts. When the source has been read, ask each student to complete the top row in Blackline Master #2.3 using information found in the document. Discuss sample responses to each question. Possible responses include:

 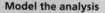

	Was it directly linked to the event (not simply accidental?)	Did it contribute to the event's direction and intensity?	Would the event have been less likely to occur if the factor had been missing?
Cause: **The *War Measures Act*** ☑ immediate ☐ underlying	*The passing of a law at the start of World War I, the War Measures Act, gave government legal justification to restrict the rights of Canadians. World War I internment was a direct consequence of the passing of the act.*	*The War Measures Act gave the Canadian government extraordinary and unprecedented powers to deny their rights to Canadians deemed a threat.*	*Government would not have had the legal power to deny rights and intern Canadians.*

Distribute the source documents

4. When it is clear that students understand the task, ask them to form groups of three. Provide each group with a copy of the following six primary and secondary sources found in the "Reasons for World War I internment" set of History docs on The Critical Thinking Consortium website:

    •   Primary source #2: Report on Iwan Milan

    •   Primary source #6: Arrest of Ukrainian socialists

    •   Primary source #7: Enemy aliens

    •   Secondary source #1: Motivations and justifications for internment

    •   Secondary source #2 Economic misfortune

    •   Secondary source #3: Divided loyalties

Explain the process

5. Encourage each group of students to collectively read one document at a time, discuss the contents, and identify any causes or information about causes contained in the document. Direct students individually to record relevant ideas in the appropriate spaces on their own copy of Blackline Master #2.3.

Determine the three most important causes

6. After jointly completing their analysis of all six documents, invite students individually to determine the three most important causes of World War I internment. Ask students to assess the influence of the causes they examined in light of the three criteria discussed above (directly linked, contributed and more likely).

Share conclusions

7. Invite a selection of individuals to share their conclusions with the rest of the class, indicating the three most important causes and their justifications for their choices based on the criteria. After various individuals have reported, provide an opportunity for students to reassess their original conclusions in light of what they have heard from others. Invite students who were persuaded to change their ranking to explain the reasons for the shift in their thinking.

1. Assess each student's completed version of Blackline Master #2.3 using the criteria in the assessment rubric found on *Assessing the causal analysis* (Blackline Master #2.4).

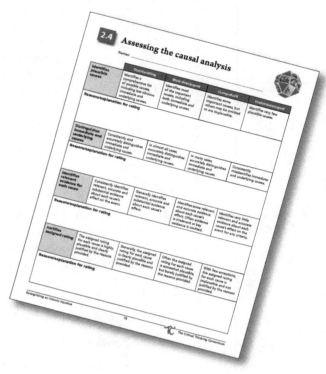

What were the camps like?

3

Critical Challenge

Critical tasks

A. Draw historically plausible conclusions about the experiences of Ukrainians and other Europeans while they were interned in Canada during World War I.

B. Write a letter from the point of view of an adolescent internee explaining his/her experience of internment.

Overview

In this three-part challenge, students learn about the experiences of those who were interned during the World War I era. Students are introduced to the idea of historical perspective-taking using an example of postal services in the nineteenth century. They consider the difference between presentism and historical perspective-taking and learn about three strategies to help in adopting a historical perspective. Students then examine various primary and secondary sources to learn about life in the internment camps from an internee's perspective. They record relevant details from the sources, draw possible conclusions and summarize what they have learned about internee's experiences. Drawing upon these findings, students write a letter from the point of view of a teenager at the time explaining the experience.

Objectives

Broad understanding

Students will appreciate the incredible hardship and suffering internees endured as a result of the harsh conditions in the internment camps.

Requisite tools

Background knowledge
- knowledge of the living and working conditions in internment camps

Criteria for judgment
- criteria for historical perspective-taking that identifies many relevant details, offers plausible and imaginative conclusions, and provides a full and realistic summary

Critical thinking vocabulary
- perspective-taking
- presentism

Thinking strategies
- activity sheet

Habits of mind
- open-mindedness

Source documents

Daily life in World War I internment camps

TC² website (History Docs): http://sourcedocs.tc2.ca/history-docs/
    topics/world-war-i-internment/reasons-for-ww-i-internment.html

Primary source #1: Internees working on a road

Primary source #2: Report on internment activities

Primary source #3: A report of complaints

Primary source #4: Prisoner on a stretcher

Primary source #5: Censored letter from an internee

Secondary source #6: Internment camp living conditions

Secondary source #7: Inspection of Spirit Lake camp

Activity sheets

Identifying historical perspective   Blackline Master #3.1

Briefing sheets

Background on Canada's
    first national internment operations   Blackline Master #1.3

Videos

Historical perspective

TC² website (Thinking about history: Video resources):
    http://tc2.ca/history.php

Historical significance

TC² website (Thinking about history: Video resources):
    http://tc2.ca/history.php

Internee descendants

Canadian First World War Internment Recognition Fund website
    (YouTube video series):
    http://www.internmentcanada.ca/pop-video4.html

Assessment rubrics

Assessing historical perspectives   Blackline Master #3.2

Assessing a historically
    realistic account   Blackline Master #3.3

The communities affected by the internment operations include Ukrainians, Bulgarians, Croatians, Czechs, Germans, Hungarians, Italians, Jews, various people from the Ottoman Empire, Polish, Romanians, Russians, Serbians, Slovaks, Slovenes, among others of which most were Ukrainians and most were civilians.

Suggested Activities

Present the sample scenario

1. Explain that students will soon attempt to get an insider's view of what it would have felt like to be caught up in the internment operations. To help students appreciate the challenges of trying to understand the mindset of people living in a different time, present the following scenario:

   - In 1858 people living in the British colony of Vancouver Island waited four to five months to receive a response to a letter sent from Victoria to London, England. This meant that important news from friends and family or advice and instructions from superiors took almost half a year to arrive.

   - Invite students to speculate briefly with a partner on what it might have been like for people in the past to wait this length of time before receiving return correspondence from the home country.

Discuss students' initial responses

2. Many students may react to the sample scenario from a modern-day perspective influenced by their experiences living at a time of instantaneous access to world news via Twitter, Facebook, cell phones, Skype and e-mail. When responding with a modern-day lens, students may suggest that the colonists might have:

   - been frustrated by having to wait so long to hear news from their homeland;

   - thought that this method of communication was inefficient and needed to be improved;

   - felt very isolated because it took so long to receive news from England.

Contrast historical perspective with presentism

3. Explain that adopting an historical perspective is not a matter of thinking how students personally would have felt in this situation but how the people at the time would likely have felt. One of the primary obstacles to historical perspective-taking is "presentism," the tendency to interpret the past according to present-day values, beliefs and experiences. When studying history, students often use modern-day lenses that distort the past and what it meant for the people living at the time. Invite students to think back to their initial responses to postal services in 1858. Which of their comments were indicative of a presentist perspective? Which were sensitive to a historical perspective?

Introduce strategies to use in historical perspective-taking

4. In trying to nurture historical perspective-taking, encourage students to consider three strategies:

   - *anticipate different beliefs and values:* Don't presume that historical attitudes, values and beliefs are identical to those that people currently hold.

   - *expect different conditions:* Sensitively imagine the realities of the time to understand what would seem unfamiliar (or very familiar) now but would be commonplace (or foreign) back then.

Reconsider initial reactions

• **attend to different meanings:** Be attentive to the fact that words and gestures may not have had the same meanings or connotations in the past as they do now.

5. Illustrate the application of these strategies by presenting additional information about mail service at the time:

   • Although mail service between Victoria and London in 1858 was still measured in months, it had improved greatly in the preceding decade. The turn-around time had been reduced by almost half, thanks to improvements in transportation, especially in the novel application of steam power to ocean transport.

6. Invite students to reconsider the historical conditions and the colonists' likely beliefs and perceptions associated with a four- to five-month wait when receiving a response to a letter (reduced from an almost year-long wait). Individually or in groups, ask students to share their responses. Possible responses may include:

Prevailing conditions	*There was very limited communication with the outside world.*
	People would not have had access to any digital technologies.
Beliefs and perceptions	*People might feel pleased to receive such a quick (relatively-speaking) response.*
	People might feel that the speed of communication was much improved compared to a decade earlier.
	People might feel less isolated and more connected to people in England than they felt previously.
	Instead of viewing a letter as "snail mail," old-fashioned and slow, people may have looked upon mail as exciting news and as a marvel of "modern" technology.

7. Invite students to share one idea that has changed from their initial thoughts about the reactions of people in the mid-nineteenth century towards the speed of the postal service.

Reinforce understanding of historical perspective-taking

8. OPTIONAL: To further explore this concept, invite students to watch the short video, *Historical perspective-taking*, found on The Critical Thinking Consortium website. Discuss the examples and the factors explained in this video.

Provide historical context to World War I internment

1. Inform students that they are now to consider the internees' experiences in the internment camps during World War I. If students have not completed other Critical Challenges in this book, provide some historical context for this event. You may wish to review what students already know, and then assign one or more of the following activities:

    *   view two short videos on the World War I internment: *Historical significance*, on The Critical Thinking Consortium website, and *Internee descendants*, on the Canadian First World War Internment Recognition Fund website.

    *   read the briefing sheet, *Background on Canada's first national internment* (Blackline Master #1.3).

Model the analysis

2. Inform students that they will now examine various primary and secondary sources in order to try to better understand how the internees might have felt. Before students begin, you may wish to model the task using the sample image, *Internees working on a road*. Direct students to look for obvious and less-obvious clues about the prevailing conditions and beliefs/perceptions associated with the camps. As suggested below, record ideas on the board under the heading, "Clues." Be sure that the details are relevant to the group's perspective. Record students' tentative conclusions about the group's experiences in a second column with the heading, "Conclusions." If students are not certain about their conclusions, encourage them to qualify their statements with words such as maybe, might or perhaps.

Clues about beliefs and prevailing conditions	Possible conclusions about the group's experience of the event
Internees are performing hard labour. Their body language suggests that the work was mundane and tedious. *Internees are constantly being monitored by guards.* *Only men appear to be doing construction.*	*Life in the camps is very harsh for internees.* *Internees have few rights and have lost their freedom.* *Families were split up when men were sent to internment camps.*

Review the criteria for historical perspective-taking

3. Distribute a copy of the rubric *Assessing historical perspective* (Blackline Master #3.2) and discuss the following criteria:

   - *identifies many relevant details,* including less obvious details that indicate the beliefs, conditions and meanings of the time;

   - *offers plausible and imaginative conclusions* that are consistent with one or more clues in the historical documents about the experiences and reactions;

   - *provides a full and realistic summary* of their conclusions, with reasons why their findings are grounded in historical facts and are not the result of a presentist perspective.

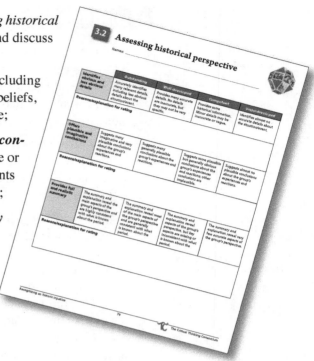

Distribute the source documents

4. When it is clear that students understand the task, ask them to form groups of three. Provide each group with a copy of the following six primary and secondary sources found in the "Life in the Internment Camps" set of History docs on The Critical Thinking Consortium website:

   - Primary source #2: Report on internment activities
   - Primary source #3: A report of complaints
   - Primary source #4: Prisoner on a stretcher
   - Primary source #5: Censored letter from an internee
   - Secondary source #6: Internment camp living conditions
   - Secondary source #7: Inspection of Spirit Lake camp

Explain the process

5. Distribute copies of *Identifying historical perspective* (Blackline Master #3.1) to each student. Explain to students that they can use this sheet to record information about internment conditions and beliefs, and draw conclusions about the internees' likely experiences and reactions. Encourage each student group collectively to read one document or image at a time, discuss the contents, and identify any clues about the camps. Based on these clues, students may draw conclusions about how people at the time would likely have felt about the internment experience. Direct students individually to record relevant ideas in the appropriate spaces on their own copy of Blackline Master #3.1. After students have recorded details and possible

conclusions from all of the assigned pages, direct them to summarize their findings about the internment experience from the people who endured it on the bottom of Blackline Master #3.1

Assess the completed analysis

6. When student have finished their analyses of the assigned sources, assess their completed copies of Blackline Master #3.1 using the rubric found on Blackline Master #3.2. Based on feedback from your assessment, encourage students to locate additional information about the event or to review some of the previously analyzed sources.

Session Three

Introduce the historically realistic letter

1. Inform students that their next task is to assume the role of a teenager and write a historically realistic letter to a relative, a newspaper editor, a government official or another historical person explaining the experiences and reactions associated with being interned. Encourage students to portray the historical perspective of a young person writing at the time. You may want to share copies of the rubric found on *Assessing a historically realistic account* (Blackline Master #3.3) with students. Explain the two criteria for the assignment:

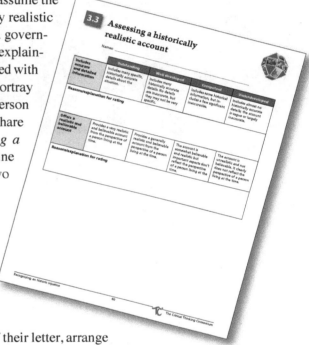

- offer accurate and detailed information about the situation;

- provide a realistic and believable account written from the perspective of a young person living at the time.

Discuss the lessons learned

2. When students have completed a draft of their letter, arrange for them to share it with another student. As a class, discuss the difficulties of adopting a historical perspective. In light of what they have just learned, encourage students to revise their letter prior to submitting it for assessment.

Assessment

1. Assess students' accounts of the experience of the internment camps represented in their revised letter using the rubric found on Blackline Master #3.3.

25 degrees below under Rundle Mountain, Banff.

Source: *In Fear of the Barbed Wire Fence: Canada's First National Internment Operations and the Ukrainian Canadians, 1914-1920*. Ed. Lubomyr Luciuk. Kingston: Kashtan Press, 2001. p. 71.

What was the impact of internment on individuals?

Critical Challenge

Critical tasks

A. Identify the obvious and less obvious direct and indirect consequences that resulted from internment during World War I.

B. Rate the legacy of the internment operations on the affected communities in terms of psychological/emotional, social/cultural, economic and political/legal impact.

Overview

In this two-part challenge, students identify and assess the direct and indirect consequences of internment on Ukrainians and others in Canada. Students learn to recognize when something is the consequence of a prior event, and to distinguish consequences that follow directly from an event from those that are indirect. Students create a web of effects to illustrate the direct and indirect consequences resulting from an event in their own lives. They then turn their attention to the consequences of Canada's first national internment operations. Using various sources, students identify the various direct and indirect consequences of World War I internment, and classify the consequences into four categories: psychological/emotional, social/cultural, economic and political/legal. Finally, students rate the severity of the impact of each category of consequence.

Objectives

Broad understanding

Dramatic historical events, such as the internment that occurred during World War I, can have profound and varied effects on many people that may last for generations.

Requisite tools

Background knowledge
- knowledge of the obvious and less-obvious direct and indirect consequences that resulted from internment during World War I

Criteria for judgment
- criteria to measure the severity of consequences including:
  - *depth:* How deeply felt or profound were the consequences?
  - *breadth:* How widespread were their impact?
  - *duration:* For how long were the consequences felt?

Critical thinking vocabulary
- direct and indirect consequences
- primary and secondary sources

Requisite tools

Thinking strategies
- web of effects
- impact assessment report

Habits of mind
- empathetic thinking

Required Resources

Source documents

Effects of World War I internment on Ukrainians

Primary source #2: Diary of commanding officer at the Castle Mountain internment camp

Primary source #5: Release certificate for William Doskoch

Primary source #6: Great War Veterans Association parade

Primary source #7: Letter to editor

Primary source #8: A descendant remembers

Primary source #10: Ukrainian Canadian economic losses during World War I

Ukrainian life in Canada after internment, 1920–1946

Primary source #2: Occupational and economic development

Primary source #4: Assimilation and prejudice

Activity sheets

Web of effects	Blackline Master #4.1
Impact assessment report	Blackline Master #4.2

Briefing sheets

Assessing direct and indirect consequences	Blackline Master #4.3

Assessment rubrics

Assessing the impact	Blackline Master #4.4

The communities affected by the internment operations include Ukrainians, Bulgarians, Croatians, Czechs, Germans, Hungarians, Italians, Jews, various people from the Ottoman Empire, Polish, Romanians, Russians, Serbians, Slovaks, Slovenes, among others of which most were Ukrainians and most were civilians.

Suggested Activities

Distinguish a "consequence" from an "afterward event"

1. Remind students that a consequence is a result or effect of an action, event or condition. Explain that just because an event occurred after another event it does not mean that the subsequent event is a consequence of the first event. In order to qualify as a consequence, the second event must result from or be caused by the earlier event. For example, if a teenager left the house angry after having a dispute with her boyfriend and then got in a car accident, it is uncertain whether the car accident was a consequence of the quarrel. We would need to determine whether the accident simply happened after the fight, or whether the fight distracted or upset the teenager in such a way as to contribute to the accident.

Using evidence to identify consequences

2. When identifying the consequences of an event or action, it is important to provide evidence that links one event to another. For example, to say that the accident was a consequence of the teenager being upset, there would need to be evidence that the argument, more than the road conditions, visibility or the speed the car was travelling at, was a key factor in the accident. Provide students with a specific action (for example, a teacher walks into the classroom) and invite students to suggest the possible events that may follow (such as, students become silent, one student sneezes, a noise is heard from outside the classroom, several students start reading their textbook). Ask students to suggest the kinds of evidence that would be required to determine whether or nor the follow-up events were consequences of the initial action. For example, we would need evidence about the reasons why students stopped talking to connect this to the teacher's arrival. Is there evidence that they even noticed the teacher? Were whispers heard among students to keep quiet because the teacher had arrived?

Explain direct and indirect consequences

3. Explain that some consequences flow immediately or directly from an event and other consequences are the result of a chain of events. Returning to the example of the car accident, suggest that it may be possible for there to be a trail of consequences from the dispute that directly led to the accident. Invite students to speculate on the range of possible events that resulted from the fight (for example, the driver was angered by the fight, called her mother to complain, was distracted while talking on the phone, and in so doing missed the turn in the road and smashed into a tree). Record these in a list on the board. Invite students to draw the links from the fight to the subsequent accident. The initial consequence of the fight (getting angry) is the direct consequence. The rest of the events are indirect consequences. Explain the following terms:

- *Direct consequences* are the immediate results of a situation (for example, bleeding is a direct consequence of cutting a finger, feeling cold is a direct consequence of going outside in the winter).

- *Indirect consequences* emerge as a result of a direct consequence and of other indirect consequences. For example, staining one's shirt with blood is an indirect consequence of cutting a finger. If a man was denied entry to a fancy restaurant because of his bloody shirt, this result would also be an indirect consequence of cutting his finger.

Apply the concepts to their own lives

4. Invite students to choose an important event that happened in their life or recently in the school. Distribute a copy of *Web of effects* (Blackline Master #4.1) to each student or group of students. Invite them to identify several direct consequences of that important event, and for each direct consequence to think of several indirect consequences. In exploring the consequences of the initial event, remind students that events often have unintended consequences, and while we can identify some consequences, it may take years or even a lifetime to reveal others. Encourage students to provide evidence that explains the link between the suggested direct consequences with the initial action, and to link the suggested indirect consequences to each other.

Self-assess the web of personal consequences

5. Distribute a copy of the rubric found on *Assessing direct and indirect consequences* (Blackline Master #4.3). Ask students to work with a partner to review the completed copy of Blackline Master #4.1 in light of the criteria described in the rubric. Review any issues that students may not have understood.

Reinforce the concept of consequences

6. OPTIONAL: Invite students to watch the short video, *Cause and consequence*, found on The Critical Thinking Consortium website. Discuss the examples and the factors explained in this video.

Introduce the first critical task

7. Inform students that they will now explore the consequences of Canada's first national internment operations for those who were interned. They will examine historical evidence from various primary sources in order to draw conclusions about the breadth, depth and duration of the impact of this injustice. Distribute another copy of *Web of effects* (Blackline Master #4.1) to each student. Invite students as they work through the various sources to record the direct and indirect consequences on this sheet. Remind students to ignore subsequent events that may have occurred after the internment operations were concluded but that are not consequences of the internment. Encourage students to recognize that indirect consequences can give rise to further consequences. The important point is not to correctly label every consequence but to understand that a particular event can have ripple effects over time.

8. When it is clear that students understand the task, divide them into groups of four. Provide each group with a copy of the following eight primary sources found in "Effects of World War I internment on Ukrainians" and "Ukrainian life after internment, 1920–1946" in History docs on The Critical Thinking Consortium website:

Effects of World War I internment on Ukrainians
- Primary source #2: Diary of commanding officer at Castle Mountain internment camp
- Primary source #5: Release certificate for William Doskoch
- Primary source #6: Great War Veterans Association parade
- Primary source #7: Letter to editor
- Primary source #8: A descendant remembers
- Primary source #10: Ukrainian Canadian economic losses during World War I

Ukrainian life after internment, 1920–1946
- Primary source #2: Occupational and economic development
- Primary source #4: Assimilation and prejudice

9. Arrange for each student in a group of four to analyze two of the eight documents and to share all the relevant information with the other members of their group. Encourage the other students to make notes on the key ideas and to offer additional comments that might add to the discussion. When each group has discussed all eight documents, ask students individually to record the important direct and indirect consequences and supporting evidence on their own copy of Blackline Master #4.1.

Session Two

1. Assess each student's identification of the indirect and direct consequences reported on *Web of effects* (Blackline Master #4.1) using the rubric found on *Assessing direct and indirect consequences* (Blackline #4.4). Encourage students to add to their web of consequences based on the assessment feedback.

2. Explain to students that events can have differentiated consequences. These can vary in their psychological/emotional, social/cultural, economic and political/legal ramifications. Provide the following definitions of these categories:
   - *psychological/emotional:* relating to the mental well-being or feelings and emotions of persons (motivation, feeling, awareness);
   - *social/cultural:* relating to the quality of the interactions with others and the ability to take part in daily events involving others;
   - *economic:* relating to their ability to earn and enjoy a livelihood, and to the conditions in which they work;
   - *political/legal:* relating to or concerned with their rights and freedoms as citizens and the involvement or influence on them by government and the legal system.

Invite several students to share the most important consequences they identified. As a class, identify which category each consequence falls into. Remind students that some consequences may affect more than one category. Advise students that when this occurs, they should select the category that best represents the consequence.

Consider the severity of consequences

3. Explain to students that not all consequences have the same impact. Consequences can vary in their severity. When considering the impact of the consequences, invite students to consider three criteria:

   - *depth:* How deeply felt or profound were the consequences?
   - *breadth:* How widespread were their impacts?
   - *duration:* For how long were the consequences felt?

   Share a few examples of the consequences that students identified and discuss the depth, breadth and duration of each.

Categorize and rate the consequences

4. Distribute a copy of *Impact assessment report* (Blackline Master #4.2). Explain that students are to divide the consequences of the internment into the four categories (psychological/emotional, social/cultural, economic, political/legal) to determine the area where the internment had its greatest impact. Encourage students to identify as many as five consequences for each category, and to list these in the left-hand column on Blackline Master #4.2. Students are then to assess the collective severity of the positive or negative impact of each category on a scale from extremely positive (+3) to extremely negative (-3). If needed, direct students to refer back to the source documents or to confer with fellow students to collect evidence to support their rating.

Share conclusions

5. Divide students into groups of three or four and invite them to share their answers with the other members of their group. Ask them to indicate which category of consequences was the most severe, and explain why. Invite each group of students to share their responses with the rest of the class.

Evaluate the impact report

6. Assess each student's evidence of and rating for the impact of the consequences reported on *Impact assessment report* (Blackline Master #4.2). Use the rubric found on *Assessing the impact* (Blackline Master #4.4).

How did internment change the communities?

Critical tasks	A. Identify the similarities and differences between the political, social and economic conditions of the communities affected by internment before and after World War I.
	B. Identify the most important similarity and difference between the pre- and post-war periods.
Overview	In this two-part challenge, students investigate the continuities and changes in conditions experienced by Ukrainian Canadians before and after World War I. Students begin by tracking similarities and differences at two comparison points in their own lives: primary school and secondary school. After discussing criteria that can be used to assess their relative importance, students identify the most important similarity and most important difference between these two periods in their lives. Students work in groups to analyze primary and secondary sources to obtain information about the political, social and economic conditions experienced by Ukrainian Canadians before and after World War I internment. They identify a range of similarities and differences and identify the most important of these in the pre- and post-war periods.

Objectives

Broad understanding	The World War I era internment operations had a significant impact on a number of affected communities.
Requisite tools	**Background knowledge** • knowledge of the the conditions of life in Canada for Ukrainians before and after World War I **Criteria for judgment** • criteria for judging whether a change is important (for example, makes a dramatic difference in daily functioning, is not easily reversed, affects a large number of people, things or events) • criteria for judging whether a continuity is important (for example, makes little if any difference in what happens, involves key aspects of peoples' lives, affects a large number of people, things or events) **Critical thinking vocabulary** • continuity and change **Thinking strategies**

Required Resources

Source documents

Conditions for early Ukrainian immigrants

TC² website (History docs): http://sourcedocs.tc2.ca/history-docs/topics/immigration/conditions-for-early-ukrainian-immigrants.html

Primary source #2: Myron Kostaniuk reflects

Primary source #4: Mary Prokop's story

Primary source #5: "It must be thoroughly disheartening…"

Primary source #7: Interview with Mary Romaniuk

Secondary source #3: Religious life of Ukrainian immigrants

Secondary source #4: Ukrainian Canadian politics

Ukrainian life after internment

TC² website (History docs): http://sourcedocs.tc2.ca/history-docs/topics/world-war-i-internment/ukrainian-life-after-internment-1920-1946.html

Primary source #2: Great War Veterans Association parade

Primary source #4: Assimilation and prejudice

Primary source #6: Born a Bohunk

Primary source #8: Ukrainian Canadian cultural festival

Primary source #9: A letter from a farmer

Secondary source #3: Ukrainians in Canadian political life

Activity sheets

Identifying similarities
and differences　　　　　　Blackline Master #5.1

Judging important differences
and similarities　　　　　　Blackline Master #5.2

Briefing sheets

Background on Canada's
first national internment operations　Blackline Master #1.3

Videos

Historical significance

TC² website (Thinking about History: Video resources)
http://tc2.ca/history.php

Internee descendants

Canadian First World War Internment Recognition Fund website
(YouTube video series): http://www.internmentcanada.ca/pop-video4.html

Continuity and change

TC² website (Thinking about History: Video resources)
http://tc2.ca/history.php

Assessment rubrics

Assessing the comparisons
and judgments　　　　　　Blackline Master #5.3

Suggested Activities

Introduce continuity and change

1. Introduce the concepts of continuity and change by indicating that you will soon ask students to think of aspects of their lives that have remained the same since they were in primary school and those that have changed since then. As a class, brainstorm categories of life experiences to compare (such as school life, home life, relationships). Explain that you want students to think of examples of similarities and differences within each of these categories. To illustrate what you require of them, suggest several actual or hypothetical examples from your own life experiences. Record your responses in a chart such as the one shown below.

Comparing life at age 6 and 16

Similarities	Differences
Relationships *Many of my closest relationships are with the same groups of people: my parents, siblings, my school friends.*	*People who were my best friends then are no longer my closest friends.*
School life *Regular school hours are very similar now to what they were when I was 6. Classes began around 9:00 am and finished around 3:00 pm.*	*The level of difficulty of lesson materials has changed significantly since primary school.*
Home life *Home remains the place where the majority of my meals are eaten and leisure time is spent.*	*I now have significant responsibility over my eating, sleeping and leisure schedule at home.*

Explore continuity and change in their own lives

2. Ask students to complete *Identifying similarities and differences* (Blackline Master #5.1) individually or in groups. Students are to record the agreed-upon categories and list as many similarities and differences in each category as they can. After completing this activity, invite students to share their observations in small groups or with the entire class. Draw out from the discussion that in all aspects of their lives, some things are changing, while other things are staying the same.

5.1 Identifying similarities and differences

Introduce criteria for judging importance

3. Invite students to consider whether all of the similarities and differences between the two time periods are equally important. For example, is moving to a new city or country a bigger change in one's life than modifications in hairstyles over the years? Introduce the following criteria for determining whether some similarities and differences are more important than others.

- Criteria for identifying an important change:
    - *substantial effect* (has a dramatic difference in daily functioning)
    - *relatively permanent* (is not easily reversed)
    - *spread difference* (affects a large number of people, things or events)

- Criteria for identifying an important continuity:
    - *substantial constancy* (makes little if any difference in what happens)
    - *relatively important* (involves key aspects of peoples' lives, not a trivial similarity)
    - *widespread constancy* (affects a large number of people, things or events).

Judge important aspects in students' lives

4. Distribute a copy of *Judging important differences and similarities* (Blackline Master #5.2) to individuals or pairs of students. Explain that they are to identify three significant differences and three significant similarities in their lives between primary and secondary school. They should then provide evidence related to the criteria discussed above for each aspect. Finally, ask students to use these criteria to judge the most important difference and the most important similarity. After completing this activity, invite students to share their conclusions in small groups or with the entire class.

Self-assess the analysis of continuity and change

5. Distribute a copy of the rubric found on *Assessing the comparisons and judgments* (Blackline Master #5.3). Ask students working in pairs to review the completed copies of Blackline Masters #5.1 and #5.2 in light of the criteria described in the rubric. Review any issues that students may not have understood.

6. OPTIONAL: For further explanation of this concept, invite students to watch the short video, *Continuity and change*, found on The Critical Thinking Consortium website. Discuss the examples and the factors explained in this video.

7. Inform students that they will now consider the changes and constants related to the conditions of Ukrainian Canadians when they first migrated to Canada in 1891 and after they suffered the internment experience during World War I. If students have not completed other Critical Challenges in this book provide some historical context for this event. You may wish to review what students already know, and then assign one or more of the following activities:

- view two short videos on the World War I internment: *Historical significance*, on The Critical Thinking Consortium website, and *Internee descendants*, on the Canadian First World War Internment Recognition Fund website.

- Read the briefing sheet, *Background on Canada's first national internment* (Blackline Master #1.3).

Session Two

1. Inform students that their first task is to look for clues from primary and secondary sources about similarities and differences in the conditions experienced by Ukrainian Canadians between the pre- and post-World War I internment periods. Explain to students that they are to compare conditions in three areas or categories:

- *political:* concerning their rights and freedoms as citizens and the involvement or influence on these by government and the legal system;

- *social:* concerning the quality of their interactions with others and the ability to take part in the daily events that others did;

- *economic:* concerning their ability to earn and enjoy a livelihood and the conditions in which they worked.

2. Before students begin, you may wish to model the task. Distribute the following documents to each student:

Conditions for early Ukrainian immigrants—
- Primary source #2: Myron Kostaniuk reflects

Ukrainian life after internment—
- Primary source #2: Great War Veterans Association parade

Focus of comparison: **Economic conditions**

Similarities	Differences
In both time periods, many Ukrainian Canadians worked in seasonal, labour-intensive, physically demanding, and low-paying industries.	*Labour opportunities were more varied after World War I and, while low-paying jobs persisted, wages differed from one industry to another.*

3. Offer an example to illustrate how some sources offer explicit information or enable obvious inferences about the group's conditions. Find another example where viewers must read between the lines or draw implicit inferences about the group's circumstances. Before students begin making observations and drawing inferences from the sources, discuss the following criteria:

- *effective observations*
  - include both obvious and less obvious features;
  - are relevant to the experiences of the featured group;
  - accurately reflect the various categories of experience.

- *thoughtful inferences*
  - are plausible;
  - are supported by evidence;
  - provide insight into the situation.

4. When it is clear that students understand the task, ask them to form groups of three. Provide each group with a copy of the five additional pre-internment sources found in "Conditions for early Ukrainian immigrants" and the five additional post-internment sources found in "Ukrainian life after internment" from the History docs on The Critical Thinking Consortium website:

Conditions for early Ukrainian immigrants

- Primary source #4: Mary Prokop's story
- Primary source #5: "It must be thoroughly disheartening…"
- Primary source #7: Interview with Mary Romaniuk
- Secondary source #3: Religious life for Ukrainian immigrants
- Secondary source #4: Ukrainian Canadian politics

Ukrainian life after internment

- Primary source #4: Assimilation and prejudice
- Primary source #6: Born a Bohunk
- Primary source #8: Ukrainian Canadian cultural festival
- Primary source #9: A letter from a farmer
- Secondary source #3: Ukrainians in Canadian political life

5. Invite students to study these sources looking for evidence of social, political and economic similarities and differences. Distribute three copies of Blackline Master #5.1 to each individual so they can record information for each of these areas. Encourage each group of students to collectively read one document at a time and make notes about the contents, all the while looking to see how things may have changed or remained constant between the two periods. Direct students individually to record relevant ideas in the appropriate spaces on their own copies of Blackline Master #5.1.

Share findings

1. When students have gathered and recorded the information on multiple copies of Blackline Master #5.1, arrange for a few students to share their findings with the rest of the class. Discuss with students how continuity and change are ever-present. Invite students to identify how certain experiences changed in some ways and were similar in other ways.

Judge important similarities and differences

2. Explain to students that their next task is to select the most important similarity and difference from among the changes and continuities they have noticed between the two time periods. Remind students of the criteria for judging the importance of continuity and change:

    *   *important difference:* substantial effect, relatively permanent, widespread difference;

    *   *important similarity:* substantial constancy, relatively important, widespread constancy

    Distribute a copy of Blackline Master #5.2 to each student. Explain to students that they must identify three key changes identified on the various copies of Blackline Master #5.1, and then decide which of these is the most important change. They should then repeat the process for the most important continuity. Remind students to look for evidence of importance in the primary and secondary sources.

3. Invite students to share their choices of the most important similarities and differences and the reasons for these judgments with the rest of the class. Discuss whether students were surprised by certain findings.

Assessment

1. Assess each student's identification of examples of similarities and differences and their justification for the most important similarities and differences using the rubric found on *Assessing the comparisons and judgments* (Blackline Master #5.3).

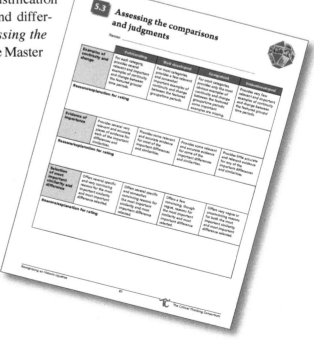

Women and children at the Spirit Lake internment camp, Quebec.

How adequately has the government responded?

Critical Challenge

Critical tasks

A. Assess official government responses to one of four legally sanctioned injustices in Canadian history.

B. Rate the adequacy or weakness of the government's official response to World War I internment and suggest possible improvements.

Overview

In this challenge, students consider the adequacy of official government responses to several of Canada's legally sanctioned injustices, including the first national internment operations. To begin, students explore a contemporary school-related scenario to learn about criteria that can be used to judge the adequacy of a response to a legally-sanctioned injustice. Working in groups, students examine official government responses to one of four historic injustices in Canada (the internment of Japanese Canadians in World War II, residential schools that Canada's indigenous peoples were forced to attend, the head tax imposed on Chinese immigrants, the refusal to allow the passengers of the *Komogata Maru* to disembark in Canada). Students compare the arguments for and against the adequacy of the official response to their assigned incident and share their findings with the rest of the class. Student rank-order these four responses in terms of their adequacy. Next, students turn their attention to the government's response to the unjust treatment of various affected communities during World War I. They rate each element of the government's response. Students communicate their conclusions with possible improvements in a letter to a government official.

Objectives

Broad understanding

Official government responses to historical injustices need to be scrutinized to determine their adequacy in making amends for the damages and suffering caused.

Requisite tools

Background knowledge
- knowledge of various historical injustices in Canada and the official government plan to redress each one

Criteria for judgment
- criteria to use to identify an adequate response (such as, sincere and full admission of responsibility, appropriate support for victims, compensation for losses, public awareness building, fair consideration of the legitimate interests of all affected parties)

Critical thinking vocabulary

Thinking strategies
- comparison charts
- rating scale

Habits of mind
- open-mindedness

Required Resources

Activity sheets
Falsely accused	Blackline Master #6.1
Judging the official response	Blackline Master #6.2
Comparing official responses	Blackline Master #6.13
Improving upon the official responses	Blackline Master #6.14

Briefing sheets
Background to Canada's first national internment operations	Blackline Master #6.3
Response to Canada's first national internment operations	Blackline Master #6.4
Background to Japanese internment	Blackline Master #6.5
Response to Japanese internment	Blackline Master #6.6
Background to Chinese head tax	Blackline Master #6.7
Response to Chinese head tax	Blackline Master #6.8
Background to the *Komagata Maru* incident	Blackline Master #6.9
Response to the *Komagata Maru* incident	Blackline Master #6.10
Background to residential schools	Blackline Master #6.11
Response to residential schools	Blackline Master #6.12

Videos
Ethical judgment
TC² website (Thinking about History: Video resources)
> http://tc2.ca/history.php

Assessment rubrics
Assessing the critique of an official response	Blackline Master #6.15
Assessing the ratings and suggestions	Blackline Master #6.16

The communities affected by the internment operations include Ukrainians, Bulgarians, Croatians, Czechs, Germans, Hungarians, Italians, Jews, various people from the Ottoman Empire, Polish, Romanians, Russians, Serbians, Slovaks, Slovenes, among others of which most were Ukrainians and most were civilians.

Suggested Activities

Present the sample scenario

1. Distribute a copy of *Falsely accused* (Blackline Master #6.1) to each student or pair of students. As a class, read the fictional scenario about a youth who is punished for bringing pills to school that were incorrectly identified as illegal drugs. Ask students to express their opinions on whether the principal's response to the false accusation was adequate or not.

Discuss criteria for identifying an adequate response

2. Ask students, either individually or in groups, to share the factors they considered when judging the adequacy of the principal's response. Invite students to compare the factors they used with the following criteria:

   - *sincere and full admission:* acknowledges the mistakes and, where warranted, exposes any intentional wrongdoing;

   - *appropriate support:* includes appropriate assistance and/or compensation for the negative experiences and consequences for the victims, their families and descendants;

   - *prevention potential:* response helps to build public awareness to avoid future injustices;

   - *fair consideration:* response fairly respects the legitimate interests of all affected parties and doesn't create new victims or ignore old ones.

Critique the principal's response

3. Distribute copies of *Judging the official response* (Blackline Master #6.2) and invite students to assemble reasons for and against the adequacy of the principal's response in light of the four criteria presented above. Place a copy on an overhead or digital projector and invite students to present their reasons, supported with evidence from the scenario. Complete the overhead transparency as a class. Finally, ask students individually to rate the adequacy of the principal's response on a scale from "much more than required" to "much less than required." Ask students to indicate their conclusions with a show of hands. Discuss the varying reasons supporting different students' conclusions.

Introduce ethical judgments in history	4. Explain to students that in history, we are often called upon to make ethical judgments of the appropriateness of the actions of governments and public officials. It is a more complicated task than what students just did when they judged the principal's response because we must be sensitive to the differing values and knowledge that existed at the historical time. It would be unfair to judge the actions of people in the past for things that they did not know about or did not consider as important as we might in the present time. Invite students to watch *Ethical judgment*, a short video prepared by The Critical Thinking Consortium. Discuss the examples and the factors explained in this video.
Introduce the four historic injustices	5. Inform students that before considering the adequacy of the government's response to the internment of thousands of Canadians of people of European descent during World War I, they will examine official government responses to four other legally sanctioned historical injustices in Canada:

- the internment of Japanese Canadians in World War II;

- the imposition of a head tax on Chinese immigrants;

- the refusal to allow the disembarkation of the *Komagata Maru* passengers;

- forced attendance in residential schools for Aboriginal people.

Distribute resources about the events	6. Provide students with another three copies of *Judging the official response* (Blackline Master #6.2) to use as they examine government responses to one of these historical injustices. Working in groups of three, direct students to learn about the nature of the government's responses using one of the following three document sets:

Japanese internment
- Background to Japanese internment (Blackline Master #6.5)
- Response to Japanese internment (Blackline Master #6.6)

Chinese head tax
- Background to Chinese head tax (Blackline Master #6.7)
- Response to Chinese head tax (Blackline Master #6.8)

Komagata Maru
- Background to the *Komagata Maru* incident (Blackline Master #6.9)
- Response to the *Komagata Maru* incident (Blackline Master #6.10)

Residential schools
- Background to residential schools (Blackline Master #6.11)
- Response to residential schools (Blackline Master #6.12)

Analyze the assigned injustice	7. Encourage students to look for evidence that supports and challenges the adequacy of the government's response to the assigned incident on each of the identified criteria. Suggest to students that when judging government responses they should assess more than the adequacy of the apology; they should also consider compensation for loss, proposed education programs, legislative protection, fact-finding initiatives, and any other elements of the response. Instruct students to reach a final conclusion about their assigned response, ranging from "much more than was required" to "much

less than was required" and to identify the three most compelling reasons for this judgment.

Session Two

Share preliminary findings

1. After jointly completing their analysis, invite students to present their findings to the rest of the class. Distribute *Comparing official responses* (Blackline Master #6.13). Rank the four government responses on the extent to which they meet the criteria for an adequate official response discussed above.

6.13 Comparing official responses

Share conclusions

2. Invite individuals to share their conclusions with the rest of the class, indicating their ranking of government responses and their justifications. After several students have reported, provide an opportunity for students to reassess their original conclusions in light of what they have heard from others. Invite students who were persuaded to change their ranking to explain the reasons for their shift in thinking.

Improve upon official response to World War I internment

3. Turn student attention back to the study of World War I internment. Distribute a copy of *Improving upon the official response* (Blackline Master #6.14) to each student and invite them to:

   a. Review the documents on World War I internment listed below.
      – *Background to Canada's first national internment operations* (Blackline Master #6.3)
      – *Response to Canada's first national internment operations* (Blackline Master #6.4)

   b. Rate each element of the response to this injustice.

   c. Suggest possible improvements to the government response.

6.14 Improving upon the official response

Write a letter of appreciation or recommendation

4. After students have reviewed each others' reasons and overall assessments, inform them that they are to draft a letter addressed to a government official that either:

   • expresses appreciation and explains why the government response is adequate;

- explains the inadequacy of the response and offers recommendations on the actions required to make proper amends; or

- expresses appreciation for what is adequate about the government's response and makes recommendations on actions required to make full amends.

Assessment

Assess the critique of the official response

1. Use the rubric found in *Assessing the critique of an official response* (Blackline Master #6.15) to evaluate students' ability to judge the adequacy of the response to the injustice as reflected in students' completed copy of Blackline Master #6.2 and their letter to the governmental official.

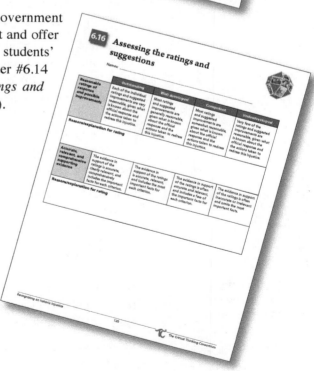

Assess the letter to the government

2. Assess students' ability to rate government responses to World War I internment and offer possible improvements as shown in students' completed copies of Blackline Master #6.14 using the rubric, *Assessing the ratings and suggestions* (Blackline Master #6.16).

What should we all know?

Critical Challenge

Critical task
Identify the ten key aspects of Canada's World War I internment operations that all Canadians should know about.

Overview
In this challenge, students decide on the most important features of Canada's World War I internment operations. Students review the key details of the event. They then consider four aspects about an injustice that are important to remember: what went on (key events), why it happened (causes), what happened as a result (consequences) and what we might learn from the event (lessons learned). Students apply these questions to a video recording of an interview about the internment operations prior to compiling the information they have learned about one of the four aspects of the event. Groups representing each of the aspects share their findings with each other and then with the entire class. Individually, students decide upon ten key ideas covering the four aspects of the injustice that all Canadians should remember.

Objectives

Broad understanding
All historical injustices are complex, multi-dimensional phenomena. It is important to remember key aspects of injustices and to honour the memory of those who have suffered past injustices in order to reduce the likelihood of similar injustices reoccurring.

Requisite tools

Background knowledge
- knowledge of causes, events, consequences and lessons learned about World War I internment

Criteria for judgment
- criteria used to select essential information (for example, is an important feature of the event, would be meaningful to those who experienced the event, helps to ensure that history doesn't repeat itself)

Critical thinking vocabulary

Thinking strategies
- data chart

Habits of mind

Activity sheets

Assembling ideas   Blackline Master #7.1

Selection of key features of the event   Blackline Master #7.2

Videos

Internee descendants

Canadian World War I Internment Recognition Fund website (YouTube video series): http://www.internmentcanada.ca/pop-video4.html)

Assessment rubric

Assessing the selection of key aspects   Blackline Master #7.3

The communities affected by the internment operations include Ukrainians, Bulgarians, Croatians, Czechs, Germans, Hungarians, Italians, Jews, various people from the Ottoman Empire, Polish, Romanians, Russians, Serbians, Slovaks, Slovenes, among others of which most were Ukrainians and most were civilians.

Suggested Activities

Introduce the task

1. Invite students to suggest what are the most important or meaningful insights or pieces of information they have learned about the World War I internment. If students had the authority to decide what every Canadian should learn about this event, what features would they include? Record their ideas on the board.

Introduce the key aspects of an injustice

2. Ask students to consider what categories or kinds of information would be most important to remember about World War I internment. Invite students to suggest categories and cluster the previously explored ideas around four key themes:

   - What went on (key events)?

   - Why did it happen (causes)?

   - What happened as a result (consequences)?

   - What might we learn from the event (lessons learned)?

Identify examples of each aspect

3. Distribute a copy of *Assembling ideas* (Blackline Master #7.1) to each student. Arrange for students to view *Internee descendants*, a short video they have already seen. While viewing, ask students to identify at least two examples of key events, causes, consequences and potential lessons learned. Invite students to share their findings with the rest of the class.

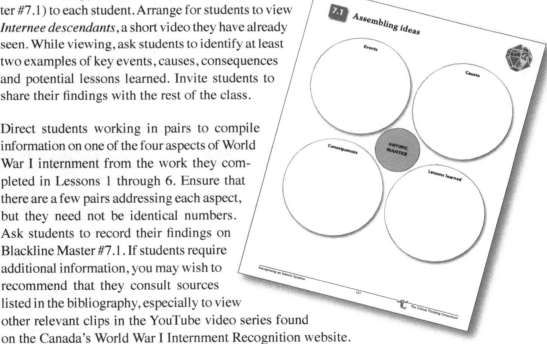

Assemble suggestions to consider

4. Direct students working in pairs to compile information on one of the four aspects of World War I internment from the work they completed in Lessons 1 through 6. Ensure that there are a few pairs addressing each aspect, but they need not be identical numbers. Ask students to record their findings on Blackline Master #7.1. If students require additional information, you may wish to recommend that they consult sources listed in the bibliography, especially to view other relevant clips in the YouTube video series found on the Canada's World War I Internment Recognition website.

Introduce criteria for selection

5. When students have compiled their information about the four aspects, invite them to share their findings and to collectively agree on ten key ideas that include all four aspects. Suggest that students consider the following criteria when deciding upon their top choices:

   - It is an important feature of the event (not a minor detail).

   - It would be meaningful to those who experienced the event.

   - It might be helpful to ensure that history doesn't repeat itself.

Share findings within affinity group

6. Arrange for all the student pairs who worked on the same aspect to assemble at a large table. (Create two groups if the number of students addressing one of the aspects is very large.) Ask students to draw spaces for each pair around the sides of a large sheet of paper and a common block in the middle. Students begin by recording their own ideas in the space directly in front of them. One by one, each pair shares what they have written. Then students discuss which of their ideas meet the criteria listed above. After consensus is reached, they record the key ideas in the centre of the paper.

Share findings with entire class

7. Arrange for each group to record all of its conclusions on the board in note form. Ask representatives from each group to explain each entry and offer reasons for the selection with the rest of the class.

Identify key features to remember

8. After the presentations are complete, invite students individually to use *Selection of key features of the event* (Blackline Master #7.2) to record and explain approximately ten key features that collectively cover all the aspects of World War I internment that all Canadians need to remember. Encourage students to justify their choices in light of the three criteria discussed above (important, meaningful and helpful).

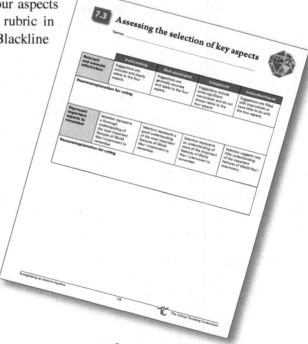

Assessment

1. Assess student understanding of the four aspects of World War I internment using the rubric in *Assessing the selection of key aspects* (Blackline Master #7.3).

Could it happen again?

8

Critical tasks

A. If the *Canadian Charter of Rights and Freedoms* had been in place at the time, which government actions associated with World War I internment operations would have been unconstitutional?

B. What restrictions or additional protections would be required today before a government could act in a similar way during a war, crisis or national emergency?

Overview

In this two-part challenge, students determine how World War I internment operations could have been different had the *Charter of Rights and Freedoms* been in place and whether such a scenario could happen again. Students consider what government actions during internment would have violated the *Charter*, if it had been in effect at the time. Students apply the "reasonable limits" conditions under Section 1 of *Charter* to determine the constitutionality of each government action. Students consider both the context of the time and the *War Measures Act*. In the second part of the challenge, students turn their attention to the restrictions or additional protections a present-day government would have to provide before it could invoke a law similar to the *War Measures Act*. Finally, students decide whether a similar situation could happen again, considering the contemporary context and current legislation.

Objectives

Broad understanding

The *Charter of Rights and Freedoms* fundamentally changed how governments can wield power during times of crisis; yet reasonable limits on these protections provide governments with the authority to restrict Canadians' rights in times of crisis, war or national emergency provided certain conditions are met.

Requisite tools

Background knowledge
- knowledge of the context of internment during World War I
- knowledge of the *Charter of Rights and Freedoms* and the reasonable limits provision
- knowledge of the federal government's actions during internment

Criteria for judgment
- criteria to determine whether a government action is a reasonable limit of rights under the *Charter* (for example, the action is pre-scribed by law, has clearly justifiable objectives and uses the least intrusive means)

Critical thinking vocabulary

Thinking strategies
- data chart

Habits of mind

Required Resources

Activity sheets

Judging the constitutionality of government actions	Blackline Master #8.1
Determining *Charter of Rights and Freedoms* protections	Blackline Master #8.2
Restricting government actions	Blackline Master #8.3

Briefing sheets

Context of the World War I internment operations	Blackline Master #8.4
Overview of the *War Measures Act*	Blackline Master #8.5
Charter of Rights and Freedoms	Blackline Master #8.6
Reasonable limits on *Charter* rights	Blackline Master #8.7
Changes to the *War Measures Act*	Blackline Master #8.8

Assessment rubrics

Assessing *Charter* conclusions	Blackline Master #8.9

The communities affected by the internment operations include Ukrainians, Bulgarians, Croatians, Czechs, Germans, Hungarians, Italians, Jews, various people from the Ottoman Empire, Polish, Romanians, Russians, Serbians, Slovaks, Slovenes, among others of which most were Ukrainians and most were civilians.

Suggested Activities

Review continuity and change and introduce the critical challenge

1. Explain to students that Canada and its laws have changed since World War I. Invite students to share examples of important changes to Canadian society and government. Remind students that continuity in history is also always present. Ask students to share constants between World War I and the present day. Ask students to consider if they think an action such as internment could ever happen again in Canada, given the changes that have occurred. Explain to students that in this critical challenge they will investigate this possibility.

Introduce the *Charter of Rights and Freedoms*

2. Explain to students that in 1982 Canada adopted a new constitution that included an important new law known as the *Charter of Rights and Freedoms*. Distribute *Charter of Rights and Freedoms* (Blackline Master #8.6) and invite students to read the various rights and freedoms that are entrenched in the constitution. Working in pairs, ask students to state in their own words what each right or freedom is protecting and to offer an example of the kinds of actions this might protect (for example, equality rights may protect an individual from being denied government services because of a physical disability). Direct students to record their examples in the margins of the briefing sheet. Ask for student volunteers to share their explanation and example for one of the provisions. Correct any obvious misunderstandings.

Introduce "reasonable limits" clause

3. Invite students to consider a scenario in which a government may have to limit or restrict certain rights. For example, ask students to consider if some rights are more important than others, such as the right to life and security over freedom of expression. Explain to students that all the rights and freedoms are subject to what is called reasonable limits under Section 1 of the *Charter*. This means that rights and freedoms are not absolute and can be restricted if certain criteria, or conditions, are met. Distribute *Reasonable limits on* Charter *rights* (Blackline Master #8.7). Invite students to consider the three conditions used for determining the reasonable limits of *Charter* rights:

   • *prescribed by law:* a limit must be embodied in an existing law or authorized by a properly delegated official or agency;

- *justified objective:* the limitation must have sufficient merit or importance to justify overriding a constitutionally protected right;

- *justified means:* the way in which the limitation is imposed must be carefully designed to achieve the objective, interfere as little as possible and causes less harm than it avoids

Practise determining *Charter* protections

4. Distribute *Determining* Charter of Rights and Freedoms *protections* (Blackline Master #8.2). Invite students in pairs to read through the two sample cases and answer the two questions for each case. After students are finished their responses, discuss the cases as a class and provide the rulings the Supreme Court of Canada made. Invite students to agree or disagree with the final rulings.

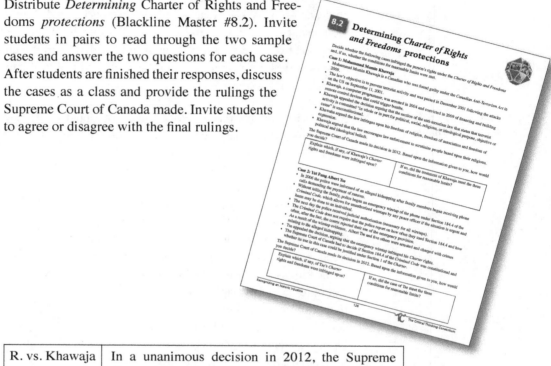

R. vs. Khawaja	In a unanimous decision in 2012, the Supreme Court of Canada ruled that the purpose of the *Anti-terrorism Act* does not infringe upon freedom of expression, religion or association, in effect making Mr. Khawaja's arrest constitutional. The court stated, "While the activities targeted by the terrorism section of the *Criminal Code* are in a sense expressive activities, most of the conduct caught by the provisions concerns acts or threats of violence." The court upheld Mr. Khawaja's sentence.
R. vs. Tse	In a unanimous decision in 2013, the Supreme Court of Canada ruled that emergency wiretap provisions found in Section 184.4 of the *Criminal Code* were not constitutional under the *Charter* right to be free from unreasonable searches (Section 8). As well, they could not be justified under the reasonable limitations clause (Section 1) as there is no accountability attached to the use of the wiretaps. The court ruled that if proper protections were put in place, emergency unauthorized wiretaps could be acceptable under the *Charter*.

Provide historical context

1. Inform students that they will now consider the federal government's actions during World War I in relation to the *Charter of Right and Freedoms*. If students are already familiar with the historical context, this step may be skipped. You may wish to review what students already know and then assign them to read *Context of the World War I internment operations* (Blackline Master #8.4).

Introduce the *War Measures Act*

2. Explain to students that the law passed to allow for internment during World War I was called the *War Measures Act*. If students have completed earlier challenges they may have some knowledge of this legislation. Explain to students that it has also been used two other times in Canada's history. Provide students with the *Overview of the* War Measures Act (Blackline Master #8.5). Inform students that understanding the law, its provisions and its use will help in completing this challenge. Invite students to identify examples of government actions during World War I internment operations that may have violated the rights and freedoms of internees. Encourage students to share their list of actions as a class.

Judge the constitutionality of the government actions

3. Distribute *Judging the constitutionality of government actions* (Blackline Master #8.1) to each pair of students. Ask students to read the list of actions in the left-hand column and compare it with their list of possible *Charter* violations.

4. Draw students' attention to the second column in Blackline Master #8.1. For each government action, ask students to first decide whether that action would have violated one of the rights and freedoms under the *Charter*, had the *Charter* been in operation at the time. Encourage students to consult Blackline Master #8.6 for a list of rights found in the *Charter*. Ask students to identify and explain which *Charter* right may have been violated.

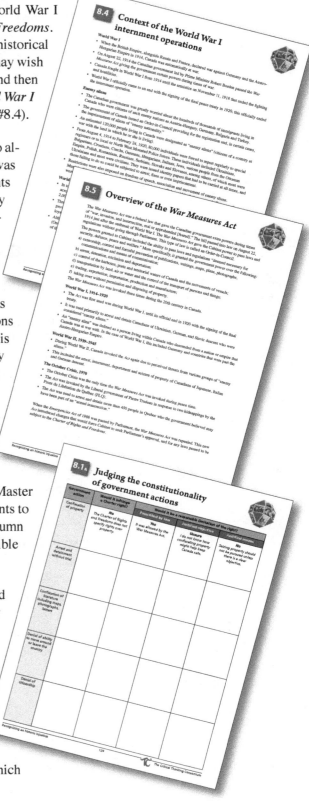

5. For each government action, ask students to consider if was a reasonable limitation of the right. Remind students to refer to the following briefing sheets when completing the activity sheet.

   • *Context of the World War I internment operations* (Blackline Master #8.4)

   • *Overview of the* War Measures Act (Blackline Master #8.5)

   • *Charter of Rights and Freedoms* (Blackline Master #8.6)

   • *Reasonable limits on Charter rights* (Blackline Master #8.7)

   Inform students they must consider the historical context of the *War Measures Act* as well as the three conditions for reasonable limits in making their judgments.

6. Invite students to share their judgments for each government action as a class. Provide an opportunity for students to revise their judgments after students have finished reporting to the class.

Session Three

1. Explain to students that the government of Canada has passed many new laws since 1970 that change how it acts during times of war, crisis or national emergency. Inform students that important changes are found in the *Emergencies Act* of 1988 and the *Anti-Terrorism Act* of 2001 and *Combatting Terror Acts* of 2013. Distribute *Changes to the* War Measures Act (Blackline Master #8.8) to students. Encourage students to identify some of the changes that would make the actions more likely to comply with the *Charter*.

2. Inform students that they will now examine what changes would need to be made to the governments' actions in order to make them constitutional. Explain to students that they can make three kinds of changes to each government action to ensure it does not violate the *Charter*:

   • add protections for certain groups or individuals (for example, cannot simply arrest people because of slight suspicion of risk);

   • remove an existing provision (for example, no longer able to take away their property);

   • limit use for certain circumstances (for example, can only be used when the danger to society is not merely possible but highly likely).

3. Ask students to consider the example of the treatment of internees in the camps. Ask students what they would need to revise in order to ensure the internees' *Charter* rights were respected while they were incarcerated. Examples might include proper food, clothing, access to communication, access to a lawyer, the expectation that they will face trial, and provision to protect their welfare from violence or inhumane conditions.

 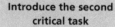

Determine the necessary revisions

4. Distribute *Restricting government actions* (Blackline Master #8.3). Invite students in pairs to provide revisions for each government action that occurred during the internment operation. Ask students to consider the following briefing sheets when making their revisions.

   • *Charter of Rights and Freedoms* (Blackline Master #8.6)

   • *Reasonable limits on Charter rights* (Blackline Master #8.7)

   • *Changes to the* War Measures Act (Blackline Master #8.8)

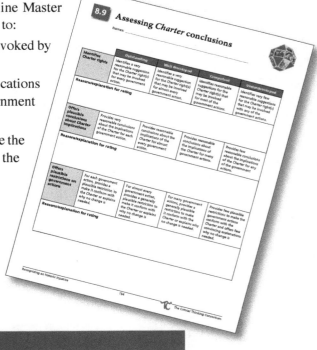

Share revisions

5. Invite students to share their revisions for each government action, indicating what *Charter* rights they kept in mind when making those revisions. After various students have reported their revisions, provide an opportunity for students to reassess their original revisions in light of what they have heard from others.

Assessment

Assess students' conclusions

1. Use the criteria in the assessment rubric found on *Assessing* Charter *conclusions* (Blackline Master #8.9) to evaluate each student's ability to:

   • identify the relevant *Charter* right invoked by each of the government's actions;

   • draw conclusions about the implications of the *Charter* for each of the government actions;

   • suggest plausible restrictions to make the government actions conform with the *Charter*.

Extension

Write a newspaper editorial

1. Invite students to write a newspaper editorial on the critical question, *Could it happen again?*

Inside the campground at Kapuskasing.

Source: *In Fear of the Barbed Wire Fence: Canada's First National Internment Operations and the Ukrainian Canadians, 1914-1920.*
Ed. Lubomyr Luciuk. Kingston: Kashtan Press, 2001. p. 37.

How can we educate others?

9

Critical Challenge

Critical tasks

A. Critique the commemorative display.

B. Create a powerful commemorative display to help educate Canadians about key aspects of World War I internment in Canada.

Overview

In this two-part challenge, students learn how they might educate Canadians about World War I internment in Canada. They begin by considering the purpose and function of commemorative displays or memorials. They develop criteria for creating a powerful commemorative, and apply these to examples from around the world. After hearing other students' critiques, each student chooses the two most powerful commemoratives. In the second part of the challenge, students design the format for a commemorative display they will create to educate Canadians about the causes, key events, consequences and lessons learned from World War I internment that they identified in Lesson 7. Students complete an initial design, receive peer feedback and refine their design. Students exhibit their completed commemorative displays for others in their school or community, explaining the selections they have made and the importance of remembering World War I internment. Finally, students write a brief reflection on what they have learned through this unit about the importance of recognizing those who have suffered past injustices.

Objectives

Broad understanding

It is important to recognize those who have suffered past injustices, and to contribute in some way to reducing the likelihood of similar injustices reoccurring.

Requisite tools

Background knowledge
- knowledge of causes, events, consequences and lessons learned about World War I internment
- knowledge of the features that characterize powerful commemorative displays

Criteria for judgment
- criteria for creating powerful commemorative displays (for example, captures important aspects of the event that the public should know about, sends a powerful message or feeling, uses interesting symbols or images)

Critical thinking vocabulary

Thinking strategies
- ranking

Habits of mind

Required Resources

Source documents

World War I internment in Canada	Blackline Master #9.2
Cambodian killing fields	Blackline Master #9.3
Holomodor	Blackline Master #9.4
Canadian soldiers in World War I	Blackline Master #9.5
Holocaust during World War II	Blackline Master #9.6
Rwandan genocide	Blackline Master #9.7

Activity sheets

Critiquing a commemorative display	Blackline Master #9.1
Ranking the commemorative displays	Blackline Master #9.8

Briefing sheets

Advice on mural making	Blackline Master #9.11

Assessment rubrics

Assessing the critique	Blackline Master #9.9
Assessing students' commemorative displays	Blackline Master #9.10

The communities affected by the internment operations include Ukrainians, Bulgarians, Croatians, Czechs, Germans, Hungarians, Italians, Jews, various people from the Ottoman Empire, Polish, Romanians, Russians, Serbians, Slovaks, Slovenes, among others of which most were Ukrainians and most were civilians.

Suggested Activities

Pre-planning

1. Depending on the format for the commemorative display that you or the students select, you may need to acquire various materials (such as Bristol board) or advise students to acquire them. If creating murals, see *Advice on mural making* (Blackline Master #9.11) for more details.

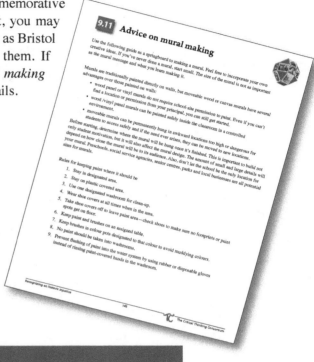

Session One

Describe purpose of educational campaigns

1. Explain to students that they have an opportunity to educate the public about this insufficiently recognized injustice in Canadian history. Ask students to share examples of public education programs they have witnessed in school assemblies that changed the way they think about an important issue. Ask students what were the most notable characteristics or features of the campaign. Record their answers on the board. Suggest to students that public education efforts are multidimensional, but what they often have in common is a powerful centrepiece display or commemorative display that leaves a lasting impact. Ask students for examples of the kinds of displays or memorials that impressed them the most.

2. Explain that memorials serve a particular purpose. Memorials are a focus for remembering something, usually a person or an event. Memorials can include landmark objects or art objects such as *sculptures*, *statues* or *fountains*, and even entire *parks*. The most common types of memorials are *gravestones* or *memorial plaques*. Also common are *war memorials* or cenotaphs that commemorate those who have died in *wars*. *Online memorials* and tributes are becoming increasingly popular. Invite students to share examples of other memorials of historical people or events they are familiar with (for example, cenotaph war memorials, statues, museum exhibits, educational centres). Ask students to consider the specific purpose of a memorial in each case.

3. Building on students' responses, suggest the following criteria for creating a powerful commemorative display:

- It captures important aspects of the event that the public should know about.

- It sends a powerful message or feeling.

- It uses interesting symbols or images.

Explain that some commemorative displays mark an event associated with a social injustice like World War I internment. These help us learn about difficult events in history, and keep alive the memory of those who have suffered. Inform students that they will examine commemorative displays that shed light on past injustices that have occurred around the world and determine which of these are the most powerful.

4. Project the image found on *World War I internment in Canada* (Blackline Master #9.2). Distribute a copy of *Critiquing a commemorative display* (Blackline Master #9.1) for each student to complete. As a class, invite students to describe the key features and to comment on this memorial in light of the criteria established earlier in the lesson. Encourage students to record their conclusions on Blackline Master #9.1.

5. Distribute another copy of Blackline Master #9.1 and a copy of one of the following commemoratives to each pair of students:

- *World War I internment in Canada* (Blackline Master #9.2)

- *Cambodian killing fields* (Blackline Master #9.3)

- *Holomodor* (Blackline Master #9.4)

- *Canadian soldiers in World War I* (Blackline Master #9.5)

- *Holocaust during World War II* (Blackline Master #9.6)

- *Rwandan genocide* (Blackline Master #9.7)

Invite each pair to repeat the process they just completed: summarize the main aspects of the injustice and critique the display in light of the criteria. Encourage students to access the internet to learn more about their featured event. Once each pair has examined its assigned commemorative display, ask them to join with the other students who critiqued the same display in order to share their conclusions. Request that each of these groups present a short summary of its analysis to the rest of the class.

6. Distribute *Ranking the commemorative displays* (Blackline Master #9.8) to each student. During each presentation, suggest that students record key ideas about each memorial on this sheet. Following the last presentation, ask students to rank the two most powerful commemoratives and explain the reasons for their ranking at the bottom of the page. Ask a sampling of students to share their rankings and their reasoning.

7. Use the rubric in *Assessing the critique* (Blackline Master #9.9) to assess students' analysis of the commemoratives recorded on Blackline Master #9.1.

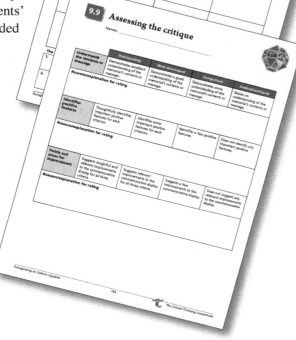

Session Two

1. Explain that students individually or in groups are now ready to create their own commemorative display of World War I internment. Explain the first task is to decide on a format for the commemorative display. Suggest several options:

- visual display (two- or three-dimensional): This could be a panel that will either be assembled into a larger class mural or mounted as an individual display.

- digital memorial: This could consist of tribute pages hosted on websites to remember a past injustice. The memorial may simply be a one-page HTML document. Content typically includes multiple photos in a gallery or slideshow plus uploaded music and videos along with memories and stories. There can be a timeline that charts a sequence of events, and there may even be a blog or journal that provides a record of emotions and feelings that are related to the main event/injustice.

- audio-visual collage: this could be presented as a PowerPoint presentation or a slide show.

- a poster or poster series.

- statue or display installation of items and artifacts that commemorate the injustice.

Invite students to select a format that interests them, allows them to effectively communicate the key information they identified in Lesson 7, and is something they are capable of doing successfully with the materials/ technology at their disposal.

Review criteria for commemorative displays

2. Remind students that while their displays may differ from each other in terms of content and design, all should satisfy the criteria for creating powerful visual displays/memorials. Review the following criteria for creating a powerful memorial with the class:

- It captures important aspects of the event that the public should know about.

- It sends a powerful message or feeling.

- It uses interesting symbols or images.

Brainstorm features contained in visual displays/memorials

3. Brainstorm different features that are often included in commemorative displays. These may include:
   - photographs;
   - letters;
   - documents;
   - artifacts;
   - statues;
   - symbols;
   - objects;
   - artwork; and/or
   - audio-visuals.

Create a preliminary design

4. Remind students that their task is to represent the key information about World War I internment (identified in Lesson 7) in their display. Encourage students to choose the most effective way to visually represent these aspects in the format they have chosen. Invite students to create a preliminary sketch or outline of their display. Encourage students to indicate the structure/organization and the main features they have chosen to use in representing the key information.

Introduce peer critique

5. Distribute another copy of Blackline Master #9.1 to each student. Explain that each student will use this form to provide feedback on a fellow student's draft design. Remind students to summarize the contents of the display and then comment on positive aspects before suggesting possible improvements for each of the criteria to create a powerful commemorative. There is no need for students to complete the summary of the injustice at the top of the sheet.

6. Allow time for each student to review another student's preliminary set of ideas/design in light of the three criteria (important details, powerful feelings, interesting symbols/images), and to explain any positive comments and suggestions.

7. Provide students with the opportunity to revise and rework their displays based on peer feedback. When all commemoratives are complete, create a class display and invite other groups to visit the display and learn about World War I internment in Canada.

8. After viewing the displays created by their classmates, ask students to respond in a short written reflection on two overarching questions:

   • Why is it important to educate the public about this injustice?

   • How can powerful commemorative displays help to reduce the likelihood of similar injustices reoccurring?

Assessment

1. Assess the final version of the displays using the rubric found in *Assessing students' commemorative displays* (Blackline Master #9.10).

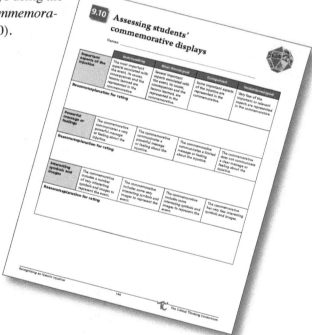

Secondary source #6: Internment camp living conditions
Secondary source #7: Inspection of Spirit Lake camp

Videos:
Historical perspective
Historical significance
Internee descendants

4 What was the impact of internment on individuals?

Blackline Masters

Online Resources

Source documents:

Effects of World War I internment

Primary source #2: Diary of commanding officer at
    Castle Mountain internment camp
Primary source #5: Release certificate for William Doskoch
Primary source #6: Great War Veterans Association parade
Primary source #7: Letter to editor
Primary source #8: A descendant remembers
Primary source #10: Ukrainian Canadian economic losses
    during World War I

Ukrainian life after internment, 1920–1946

Primary source #2: Great War Veterans Association parade
Primary source #4: Assimilation and prejudice

Video:
Cause and consequence

5 How did internment change the communities?

Blackline Masters

Online Resources

Source documents:

Conditions for early Ukrainian immigrants

Primary source #2: Myron Kostaniuk reflects
Primary source #4: Mary Prokop's story
Primary source #5: "It must be thoroughly disheartening…"
Primary source #7: Interview with Mary Romaniuk
Secondary source #3: Religious life of Ukrainian immigrants
Secondary source #4: Ukrainian Canadian politics

Videos:
Historical significance
Internee descendants
Continuity and change

Blackline Masters

1.1   Internment in Canada

Event 1

At the time that war started, there were 500,000 people living in Canada who were citizens of various countries considered enemies of the nation. Many were second-generation Canadian born and many spoke English as their primary language. During the war, a total of 80,000 of these Canadian residents were forced to register with the police, and report back to them once a month if they lived in cities, or less often if they lived in isolated places. Failure to report resulted in fines or even imprisonment.

7,762 of these Canadian residents, including 81 women and 156 children, were taken to one of 24 internment camps across Canada as enemy aliens. All of their property and money was taken by the government. Internees were forced to work, with some of this labour done without pay; however, according to law, any work completed for the advantage of the government had to be paid. The pay was low, and the work was heavy, including building roads and railways, and clearing land. Internees were divided into two classes, and the first class people were given better living conditions and food.

While some of these internment camps closed after a couple of years because there was a shortage of labour, and not enough workers to keep them running. This demand for workers also meant that the internees were parolled to private companies and sent all across Canada, without their families, and forced to work at whatever jobs they were needed for. Other camps remained in operation until 18 months after the war ended; some people lived as long as six years in these camps.

Event 2

When war broke out, there were 23,224 people of a certain ethnic origin living in Canada who were citizens of countries considered enemies of the nation. More than half of these people were second-generation Canadian born and many spoke English as their primary language. During the war, the Prime Minister publicly questioned the loyalty of these Canadians and all over the age of 16 were forced to register with the police.

A year later, all individuals of this particular heritage who lived near the ocean coastline were ordered to leave their homes. They were allowed one suitcase each; the rest of their property was turned over to the authorities. Some were made to live in cow barns for a time. Then, men over 18 were sent to work in road camps, on farms, or to POW (prisoner of war) camps surrounded by barbed wire. 12,000 women, children and elderly were transported to ghost towns, to live in conditions ill-equipped for the bitter winter. Many men were separated from their wives and children and sent to work. They were paid a small wage, and forced to pay room and board out of that wage. Their property was sold and used to pay for the costs of their internment. Some of these people were set free once the war was ended; others were deported to their ancestral country of origin.

Comparing events

	Event 1	Event 2
Who?		
What?		
Where?		
When?		
Why?		

Compare the importance of the two events: **Reasons for ranking**

❑ Event 1 is much more important than Event 2

❑ Event 1 is a little more important than Event 2

❑ Events 1 and 2 are equally important

❑ Event 1 is a little less important than Event 2

❑ Event 1 is much less important than Event 2

Background on Canada's first national internment operations

Canada's first national internment operations

Even though there was never any evidence of disloyalty on their part, thousands of people living in Canada were imprisoned needlessly and forced to do heavy labour in twenty-four internment camps located in the country's frontier hinterlands. Tens of thousands of others, designated as "enemy aliens," were obliged to carry identity documents and report regularly to the police. Many were subjected to other state-sanctioned indignities, including disenfranchisement, restrictions on their freedom of speech, movement and association, deportation and the confiscation of what little wealth they had, some of which was never returned.

Camp Otter Yoho National Park. Source: *In Fear of the Barbed Wire Fence: Canada's First National Internment Operations and the Ukrainian Canadians, 1914-1920*. Ed. Lubomyr Luciuk. Kingston: Kashtan Press, 2001. p. 60.

World War I and the post-war period (1914–1920)

During Canada's first national internment operations between 1914 and 1920, the families of those labeled "enemy aliens" were separated, their property confiscated and sold, and thousands of men were consigned to internment camps and years of forced labour in Canada's wilderness. "I say unhesitatingly that every enemy alien who was interned during the war is today just as much an enemy as he was during the war, and I demand of this Government that each and every alien in this dominion should be deported at the earliest opportunity.... Cattle ships are good enough for them." Herbert S. Clements, MP (Kent West, Ontario), 24 March 1919

25 degrees below under Rundle Mountain, Banff. Source: *In Fear of the Barbed Wire Fence: Canada's First National Internment Operations and the Ukrainian Canadians, 1914-1920*. Ed. Lubomyr Luciuk. Kingston: Kashtan Press, 2001. p. 71.

Canadians of European descent

The affected communities include Ukrainians, Bulgarians, Croatians, Czechs, Germans, Hungarians, Italians, Jews, various people from the Ottoman Empire, Polish, Romanians, Russians, Serbians, Slovaks, Slovenes, among others of which most were Ukrainians and most were civilians. "I was one of the thousands of Ukrainian Canadians rounded up as 'enemy aliens' and put in concentration camps between 1914–1920. I was born in Canada. I lived in Montreal with my parents, brother, John, and sisters, Anne and Nellie. She was just two-and-a-half when we buried her near the Spirit Lake internment camp. Canada's Ukrainians were not disloyal. Our imprisonment was wrong. We were Canadians.

Women and children at the Spirit Lake internment camp, Quebec. Source: Ukrainian Canadian Civil Liberties Association

Those who, like my parents, had come from Ukraine to Canada, came seeking freedom. They were invited here. They worked hard. They contributed to this country, with their blood, sweat and tears."

Wartime anxiety, intolerance and xenophobia

This happened even though the British Foreign Office informed Ottawa that these eastern Europeans were "friendly aliens" who should be given "preferential treatment." These men, women and children suffered not because of anything they had done but only because of who they were, and where they had come from.

Great War Veterans Association parade and rally in Winnipeg, Manitoba, June 4, 1919. Source: Archives of Manitoba, Winnipeg Strike 5 (N12296).

Where?	Nearly 9,000 men, women and children were interned in 24 camps across the country. Most internees were men, but some were women and children, who were held at Spirit Lake (near Amos, Quebec) and at Vernon, British Columbia. These civilian internees ("second class") were separated from genuine German and Austrian prisoners-of-war and then transported to the country's frontier hinterlands, where they were forced to do heavy labour under trying circumstances.

CANADA'S FIRST NATIONAL INTERNMENT OPERATIONS 1914-1920

☐ Recieving Station
○ Permanent Interment Camp
● Road-building and Land-clearing
▲ Camp Construction

© First World War Internment Recognition Fund. Used with permission.

Location of camp	Date of opening	Date of closing
Montreal, Quebec	13 August 1914	30 November 1918
Kingston, Ontario	18 August 1914	3 November 1917
Winnipeg, Manitoba	1 September 1914	29 July 1916
Halifax, Nova Scotia	8 September 1914	3 October 1918
Vernon, British Columbia	18 September 1914	20 February 1920
Nanaimo, British Columbia	20 September 1914	17 September 1915
Brandon, Manitoba	22 September 1914	29 July 1916
Lethbridge, Alberta	30 September 1914	7 November 1916
Petawawa, Ontario	10 December 1914	8 May 1916
Toronto, Ontario	14 December 1914	2 October 1916
Kapuskasing, Ontario	14 December 1914	24 February 1920
Niagara Falls, Ontario	15 December 1914	31 August 1918
Beauport, Quebec	28 December 1914	22 June 1916
Spirit Lake, Quebec	13 January 1915	28 January 1917
Sault Ste Marie, Ontario	3 January 1915	29 January1918
Amherst, Nova Scotia	17 April 1915	27 September 1919
Monashee–Mara Lake, British Columbia	2 June 1915	29 July 1917
Fernie–Morrissey, British Columbia	9 June 1915	21 October 1918
Banff–Cave and Basin, Castle Mountain, Alberta	14 July 1915	15 July 1917
Edgewood, British Columbia	19 August 1915	23 September 1916
Revelstoke–Field–Otter, British Columbia	6 September 1915	23 October 1916
Jasper, Alberta	8 February 1916	31 August 1916
Munson, Alberta–Eaton, Saskatchewan	13 October 1918	21 March 1919
Valcartier, Quebec	24 April 1915	23 October 1915

1.4 Rating historical significance

Event: _____

Criteria	Rating					Evidence
Important at the time? _Immediate recognition:_ Was it noticed at the time as having importance? _Duration:_ How long did it exist or operate?	**0** not at all significant	**1** of minor significance	**2** somewhat significant	**3** quite significant	**4** very significant	
Profound consequences? _Magnitude of impact:_ How deeply felt or profound was it? _Scope of impact:_ How widespread was it? _Lasting nature of impact:_ How lasting were its effects?	**0** not at all significant	**1** of minor significance	**2** somewhat significant	**3** quite significant	**4** very significant	
Symbolic message? _Remembered:_ Has it been memorialized? _Revealing:_ Does it represent a historical issue or trend?	**0** not at all significant	**1** of minor significance	**2** somewhat significant	**3** quite significant	**4** very significant	

Considering the ratings above, this event is:

❑ Not at all significant: not worth remembering.

❑ Individually significant: the descendants and family of the people involved should know about this event.

❑ Regionally significant: every student in the region where it occurred or who belongs to the specific group(s) affected should study this event.

❑ Nationally significant: every student in the country where it occurred should study this event.

❑ Globally significant: every student in the world should study about this historical event.

Reasons:

Assessing the rating of historical significance

Names: _____

	Outstanding	Well developed	Competent	Underdeveloped
Plausible individual and overall ratings	Each of the individual ratings and the overall assessment are highly plausible, given what historians know about the event.	Most ratings are generally plausible, given what historians know about the event.	Most ratings are some-what plausible, given what historians know about the event; a few ratings are question-able.	Very few of the ratings are plausible, given what historians know about the event.
Reasons/explanation for rating				
Accurate, relevant, and comprehensive supporting evidence	The evidence in support of the ratings is accurate, clearly relevant, and comprehensive of the important facts for each criterion.	The evidence in support of the ratings is accurate, relevant, and includes the most important facts for each criterion.	The evidence in support of the ratings is often accurate and relevant, and includes a few of the important facts for each criterion.	The evidence in support of the ratings is often inaccurate or irrelevant and omits the most important facts.
Reasons/explanation for rating				

71

2.1 Identifying the causes of the accident

Just before midnight one dark and stormy night, a man called John Smith, who worked as an engine mechanic, was sitting in an isolated cabin in the woods. As he reached for a cigarette, he noticed he had only one left. Glancing at his watch, he realized that he had just enough time to hop in his car and drive to the gas station down the road to buy cigarettes before it closed. As he pulled out of his lane onto the highway, his car was hit by his neighbour, who, returning from a long night of drinking, was unable to stop his car soon enough on the icy road. Smith was killed instantly. Later, as the townspeople were discussing the sad event, they shook their heads one after another and said, "We always knew that smoking would kill Smith." It is worth noting that local officials had long been warned of the dangers on that part of the highway, especially in winter, and yet they seemed uninterested in doing anything about it. Apparently this was because the residents of that part of the town did not have any influence with local authorities. Others wondered whether, if the impaired driving laws had been more faithfully enforced in the town, whether the neighbour who smashed into Smith would have been as drunk as he was.[1]

List the contributing factors to the accident

---

[1] Taken from *Heaven & Hell on Earth: The Massacre of the "Black" Donnellys*, part of the Great Unsolved Mysteries in Canadian History series: www.canadianmysteries.ca.

Sorting immediate and underlying causes

1. It was late at night on a dark and stormy night.

2. Perhaps because he was in a rush, John Smith didn't exercise enough caution when pulling out onto the highway.

3. This part of the highway had long been known to be dangerous and, despite warnings, the authorities had failed to do anything about it.

4. The roads were icy and difficult to drive on.

5. The neighbour who crashed into John Smith was driving while impaired from alcohol.

6. The town council was biased against the recommendations and complaints made by people in that part of the town.

7. Liquor laws in the town were not faithfully enforced by the police.

8. The neighbour who crashed into John Smith failed to consider the icy conditions on the road.

Immediate causes	Underlying causes
• Are often the most obvious and easily identified. • Typically occur just prior to the event in question. • Removal of immediate causes may not have prevented the occurrence of the event, as there may be more significant factors contributing to the event.	• Are usually less obvious and more difficult to identify. • Are often a broader underlying condition, practice, or belief and not tied to a single event. • Removal of an underlying cause may help prevent the event from occurring.

Examining causal factors

Event: _____

	Is it directly linked to the event (not simply accidental)?	Does it contribute to the event's direction and intensity?	Would the event have been less likely to occur if the factor had been missing?
Cause: ❑ Immediate ❑ Underlying			
Cause: ❑ Immediate ❑ Underlying			
Cause: ❑ Immediate ❑ Underlying			
Cause: ❑ Immediate ❑ Underlying			
Cause: ❑ Immediate ❑ Underlying			

	Is it directly linked to the event (not simply accidental)?	Does it contribute to the event's direction and intensity?	Would the event have been less likely to occur if the factor had been missing?
Cause: ❏ Immediate ❏ Underlying			
Cause: ❏ Immediate ❏ Underlying			
Cause: ❏ Immediate ❏ Underlying			

Most important contributing factors	Reasons
1.	
2.	
3.	

75

2.4 Assessing the causal analysis

Names: _____

	Outstanding	**Well developed**	**Competent**	**Underdeveloped**
Identifies plausible causes	Identifies a comprehensive list of possible causes, including less obvious immediate and underlying causes.	Identifies most of the important causes, including both immediate and underlying causes.	Identifies some important causes, but others may be omitted or are implausible.	Identifies very few plausible causes.
Reasons/explanation for rating				
Distinguishes immediate and underlying causes	Consistently and accurately distinguishes immediate and underlying causes.	In almost all cases, accurately distinguishes immediate and underlying causes.	In many cases, accurately distinguishes immediate and underlying causes.	Consistently misidentifies immediate and underlying causes.
Reasons/explanation for rating				
Identifies relevant evidence for each cause	Consistently identifies relevant, accurate and substantial evidence about each cause's effect on the event.	Generally identifies relevant, accurate and substantial evidence about each cause's effect.	Identifies some relevant and accurate evidence about each cause's effect. Often evidence is irrelevant or key evidence is omitted.	Identifies very little relevant and accurate evidence about each cause's effect on the event for any criteria.
Reasons/explanation for rating				
Justifies assigned rating	The assigned rating for each cause is highly plausible and clearly justified by the reasons provided.	Generally, the assigned rating for each cause is clearly plausible and justified by the reasons provided.	Often the assigned rating for each cause is somewhat plausible, but barely justified by the reasons provided.	With few exceptions, the assigned rating for each cause is implausible and not justified by the reasons provided.
Reasons/explanation for rating				

Identifying historical perspective

Featured group: _____

Source	Clues about beliefs and prevailing conditions	Possible conclusions about the group's experience of the event
1.		
2.		
3.		
4.		

Source	Clues about beliefs and prevailing conditions	Possible conclusions about the group's experience of the event
5.		
6.		

Summary of the group's experiences and attitudes

Names: _____

	Outstanding	Well developed	Competent	Underdeveloped
Identifies obvious and less obvious details	Accurately identifies many relevant details, including less obvious details about the situation/event.	Provides many accurate details. No details are inaccurate, but they may not be very specific.	Provides some historical information. Minor details may be inaccurate or vague.	Identifies almost no accurate details about the situation/event.
Reasons/explanation for rating				
Offers plausible and imaginative conclusions	Suggests many imaginative and very plausible conclusions about the group's experiences and reactions.	Suggests many generally plausible conclusions about the group's experiences and reactions.	Suggests some plausible but generally obvious conclusions about the group's experiences and reactions; other conclusions are implausible.	Suggests almost no plausible conclusions about the group's experiences and reactions.
Reasons/explanation for rating				
Provides full and realistic summary	The summary and explanation reveal the main aspects of the group's perspective and are highly consistent with what is known about the period.	The summary and explanation reveal most of the main aspects of the group's perspective and are generally consistent with what is known about the period.	The summary and explanation reveal aspects of the group's perspective, but key aspects are missing or inconsistent with what is known about the period.	The summary and explanation reveal very few accurate aspects of the group's perspective.
Reasons/explanation for rating				

Assessing a historically realistic account

Names: _____

	Outstanding	**Well developed**	**Competent**	**Underdeveloped**
Includes accurate and detailed information	Includes many specific, historically accurate details about the situation.	Includes many historically accurate details. No details are inaccurate, but they may not be very specific.	Includes some historical information, but includes a few significant inaccuracies.	Includes almost no historically accurate details; the account is vague or largely inaccurate.
Reasons/explanation for rating				
Offers a realistic and believable account	Provides a very realistic and believable account from the perspective of a person living at the time.	Provides a generally realistic and believable account from the perspective of a person living at the time.	The account is somewhat believable and realistic but important aspects don't reflect the perspective of a person living at the time.	The account is unrealistic and not believable. It clearly does not reflect the perspective of a person living at the time.
Reasons/explanation for rating				

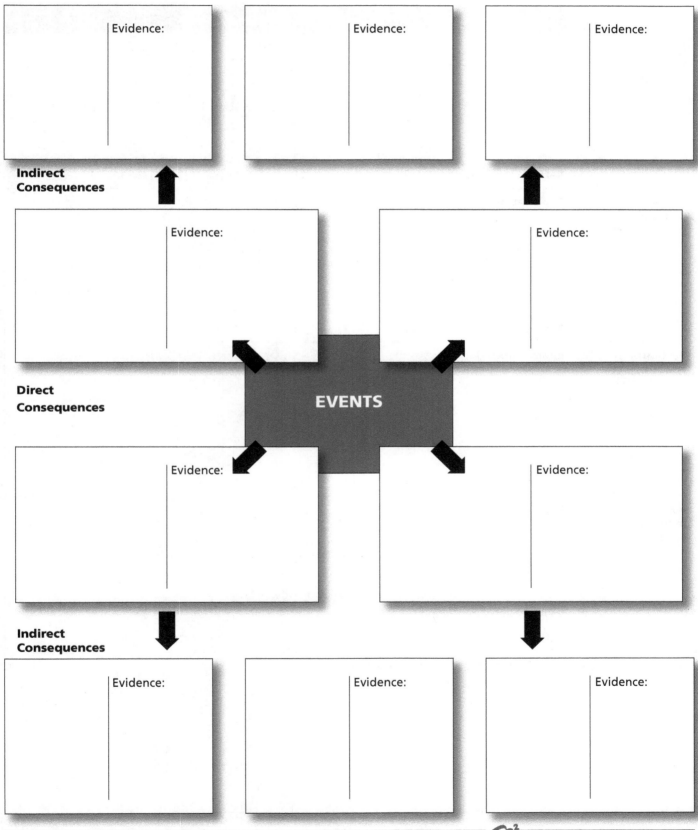

Evidence:

Evidence:

Evidence:

**Indirect
Consequences**

Evidence:

Evidence:

**Direct
Consequences**

EVENTS

Evidence:

Evidence:

**Indirect
Consequences**

Evidence:

Evidence:

Evidence:

4.2 Impact assessment report

	Depth, breadth and duration of impact						
Psychological/ emotional consequences	Explanation:						
	Rating: +3	+2	+1	0	-1	-2	-3
Social/ cultural consequences	Explanation:						
	Rating: +3	+2	+1	0	-1	-2	-3
Economic consequences	Explanation:						
	Rating: +3	+2	+1	0	-1	-2	-3
Political/ legal consequences	Explanation:						
	Rating: +3	+2	+1	0	-1	-2	-3
Overall impact (considering evidence from all categories):							

Assessing direct and indirect consequences

Names: _____

	Outstanding	Well developed	Competent	Underdeveloped
Identifies significant direct consequences	Identifies several significant direct consequences that resulted from the event with relevant supporting evidence.	Identifies a few significant direct consequences that resulted from the event with some supporting evidence.	Identifies obvious direct consequences that resulted from the event, but omits significant consequences. Little supporting evidence is provided.	Offers no direct consequences resulting from the event, or confuses direct and indirect consequences.
Reasons/explanation for rating				
Identifies significant indirect consequences	Identifies several significant indirect consequences that resulted from each direct consequence with relevant supporting evidence.	Identifies a few significant indirect consequences that resulted from each direct consequence.	Identifies a few obvious indirect consequences that resulted from each direct consequence with some supporting evidence.	Identifies no indirect consequences that resulted from the direct consequences, or confuses direct and indirect consequences.
Reasons/explanation for rating				

Assessing the impact

Names: _____

	Outstanding	Well developed	Competent	Underdeveloped
Identifies relevant and important consequences for each category	Identifies several relevant and important consequences for each category.	Identifies several relevant and important consequences for most categories.	Identifies a few obvious consequences for most categories, but misses significant consequences.	Identifies very few consequences and often classifies them into inappropriate categories.
Reasons/explanation for rating				
Supports with accurate, relevant and detailed evidence	Provides accurate and detailed evidence for the depth, breadth and duration of impact for most of the identified consequences.	Provides generally accurate evidence for the depth, breadth and duration of impact for most of the identified consequences.	Provides evidence of impact for many of the identified consequences, but some evidence is inaccurate or exaggerated.	Provides very little evidence of impact for any of the identified consequences.
Reasons/explanation for rating				
Offers plausible ratings	Provides highly plausible ratings for each category.	Provides generally plausible ratings for most categories.	Provides plausible ratings for some categories, but not all.	Provides implausible ratings.
Reasons/explanation for rating				

Identifying similarities and differences

Focus of comparison: _____

Similarities	Differences

Judging important differences and similarities

Key differences	Evidence of the importance of a change Summarize what is known about the depth of its effect, its permanence and how widespread its impact was
Explanation of the most important difference	

Key similarities	Evidence of the importance of the continuity Summarize what is known about how little difference there was, the importance of the similarity and how widespread it was
Explanation of the most important similarity	

Assessing the comparisons and judgments

Names: _____

	Outstanding	Well developed	Competent	Underdeveloped
Examples of continuity and change	For each category, provides several relevant and important examples of continuity and change between the featured groups/ time periods.	For most categories, provides a few relevant and somewhat important examples of continuity and change between the featured groups/time periods.	For most categories, provides only the most obvious examples of continuity and change between the featured groups/time periods; some important examples are missing.	Provides very few relevant and important examples of continuity and change between the featured groups/ time periods.
Reasons/explanation for rating				
Evidence of importance	Provides several very relevant and accurate pieces of evidence for each of the important differences and similarities.	Provides some relevant and accurate evidence for most of the important differences and similarities.	Provides some relevant and accurate evidence for some of the important differences and similarities.	Provides little accurate and relevant evidence for any of the important differences and similarities.
Reasons/explanation for rating				
Selection of most important similarity and difference	Offers several specific and very convincing reasons for the most important similarity and most important difference selected.	Offers several specific and somewhat convincing reasons for the most important similarity and most important difference selected.	Offers a few convincing, though vague, reasons for the most important similarity and most important difference selected.	Offers very vague or unconvincing reasons for both the most important similarity and most important difference selected.
Reasons/explanation for rating				

Falsely accused

Marcus had a terrible headache before school one day, but he didn't want to miss an important science class so he took two acetaminophen pills. His mother placed a handful of pills in a plastic bag so that he could take them at school in case his headache continued. When Marcus arrived at school he opened his locker, and began to place the bag of pills in his locker. Just at this moment, a teacher walked by. He immediately reported to the school principal, Mrs. Green, that he had seen Marcus at his locker with a bag of pills.

Mrs. Green went to Marcus' classroom, demanded that he gather all of his things and escorted him roughly to her office. Once in the office, Mrs. Green informed Marcus that school authorities had forced open his locker and found a bag of illegal drugs inside. Marcus explained that the pills were for his headache. The principal was unconvinced, suggesting instead that Marcus had brought the pills to school for the purpose of selling them to other students. She suspended Marcus from school and informed his parents and the police.

When the police arrived, they handcuffed and escorted Marcus through the crowded hallways to the police car. He was detained overnight in jail and missed a week of classes because of the principal's suspension. News of his arrest spread throughout the community. The local newspaper contained an article on illegal drugs in schools and mentioned Marcus by name.

When the test results finally arrived, they revealed that the drugs were not illegal, but common headache medication. Upon learning of this development, Mrs. Green sent a letter to Marcus' home apologizing for the misunderstanding, but suggesting that he be more careful in future about bringing suspicious-looking drugs to school without a note from his parents.

6.2 Judging the official response

Summary of the injustice(s)	Immediate and long-term consequences

Official response(s) to the injustice

Criteria identifying an adequate apology	Reasons why it may be adequate	Reasons why it may not be adequate
Sincere and full admission *Acknowledgment of the mistakes and, where warranted, exposes any intentional wrongdoing.*		
Adequate support *Appropriate assistance and/or compensation for the negative experiences and consequences for the victims and their families and descendants.*		
Prevention potential *Response helps to build public awareness and avoid future injustices.*		
Fair consideration *Response fairly respects the legitimate interests of all affected parties and doesn't create new victims or ignore old ones.*		

Overall assessment	**Reasons for assessment**
❑ Much more than was required ❑ A little more than was required ❑ Exactly what was required ❑ A little less than was required ❑ Much less than was required	1. 2. 3.

Background to Canada's first national internment operations

"Fire alarm," Cave and Basin, Banff National Park.
Source: Glenbow Museum and Archive.

Historical context

Roughly 2.5 million newcomers arrived in Canada between 1896 and 1911. A significant proportion of new immigrants came from Eastern Europe, and of these, the largest number was Ukrainian. These immigrants were actively recruited by the Canadian government, which was in search of workers to feed its growing resource and agricultural sectors. Like other immigrants, these newcomers faced many hardships and struggles in what was often an unwelcoming land. However, the outbreak of World War I profoundly altered their lives in ways they could not have imagined when they left their homeland in search of a better life in Canada.

Details about World War I internment

Having emigrated from territories under the control of the Austro-Hungarian Empire, one of Canada's enemies during World War I, immigrants from Europe and Asia Minor came under increasing suspicion. Wartime fears and anxieties led to an increase in xenophobia (intense dislike or fear of people from other countries). The passage of the *War Measures Act* (a law used in times of emergency) provided the legal basis for the federal government to deny basic rights to Canadians. This resulted in the internment of 8,579 Canadians labeled as enemy aliens. Over 5,000 were Ukrainians. In addition, 80,000 individuals were required to register as enemy aliens and to report to local authorities on a regular basis. The affected communities include Ukrainians, Bulgarians, Croatians, Czechs, Germans, Hungarians, Italians, Jews, various people from the Ottoman Empire, Polish, Romanians, Russians, Serbians, Slovaks, Slovenes, among others of which most were Ukrainians and most were civilians.

Referred to as Canada's first national internment operations, the period between 1914 and 1920 saw members of affected communities separated, their property confiscated and sold and thousands of men sent to internment camps to do years of forced labour in Canada's wilderness. These internees were subjected to harsh living and working conditions, and they were used to develop Canadian infrastructure as forced labourers. They were used to develop Banff National Park, experimental farms in northern Ontario and Quebec, steel mills in Ontario and Nova Scotia, and they toiled in the mines in British Columbia, Ontario and Nova Scotia. These development programs benefited Canadian corporations to such a degree that the internment was carried on for two years after the end of World War I.

Inside the campground at Kapuskasing.
Source: *In Fear of the Barbed Wire Fence: Canada's First National Internment Operations and the Ukrainian Canadians, 1914-1920*. Ed. Lubomyr Luciuk. Kingston: Kashtan Press, 2001, p. 37. Published with the permission of Lubomyr Luciuk.

To this date, it is unclear what the driving force for the internment was. Some have argued that it was due to "war fever" and the resulting wartime fear of people from other countries and cultures. Others point to the economic benefits of a forced labour system that provided companies with abundant cheap labour.

Significance of World War I internment

Internment during the World War I era is an example of legally sanctioned injustice, where the civil rights of targeted Canadians are denied without just cause, and entire communities are subjected to indignity, abuse and untold suffering. The *War Measures Act*, which was first implemented during World War I, provided the legal justification for the internment, and was also used as the basis for interning Japanese Canadians and others during World War II. World War I internment exposed many of the anti-immigrant feelings of the general population of the day. Internment marked the beginning of a traumatic period in the affected communities, one that would leave deep scars long after the last internment camp was closed.

Response to Canada's first national internment operations

The movement for redress and early government responses

Beginning in 1985, Canada's Ukrainian community sought official acknowledgement (recognition) and redress (to make up for past wrongs) for Canada's first national internment operations from 1914-1920. This led to the development of a campaign that focused on the government's moral, legal and political duty to redress the historical wrong. Dr. Lubomyr Luciuk, a leading member of the Ukrainian Canadian Civil Liberties Association stated:

> Yet the community's campaign for acknowledgement and redress has not, unlike that of our fellow Japanese Canadians, achieved all of its goals, despite ten years of effort. In large measure this is because those officials responsible for dealing with the Ukrainian-Canadian community's claims (and those of other communities which have brought forward redress issues) have quite deliberately and systematically attempted to dismiss and delay any resolution of the Ukrainian-Canadian case. They have reacted only when community-based initiatives have forced their hand… or when, in the weeks just before the fall 1988 and fall 1993 federal elections, their political masters felt some need to placate [to make less angry or hostile] a Ukrainian-Canadian constituency numbering over one million people. Otherwise the Ukrainian-Canadian redress issue has all but been ignored. Ottawa has used what might be referred to as a "wait and hope they go away" strategy, in no way different from the one earlier deployed against the NJAC [National Association of Japanese Canadians].

Member of Parliament Inky Mark, who proposed Bill-C331, which provided the basis for official government acknowledgement and symbolic redress of Canada's first national internment operations, 1914–1920.
Source: BRAMA, November 12, 2002.

Government recognition and the redress agreement

The efforts of those involved in the redress movement were realized on November 25, 2005, when Conservative Member of Parliament Inky Mark's Private Member's Bill C-331, *Internment of Persons of Ukrainian Origin Recognition Act*, was passed. While there was no official government apology, this act acknowledges that persons of Ukrainian origin were interned in Canada during World War I. Also, it legally required the government of Canada to take action to recognize the internment and provide funding for educational and commemorative (to remember and honour) projects.

On May 9, 2008, the Canadian government established a $10 million fund. The Endowment Council of the Canadian First World War Internment Recognition Fund uses the interest earned on that amount to fund

projects that commemorate the experience of the thousands who were interned between 1914–20. The funds are used to support educational and cultural activities that keep alive the memory of those who suffered during Canada's first national internment operations. The endowment fund is the result of 20 years of hard work by a small group of dedicated and determined members of the Ukrainian community. There were many stops and starts along the way, but these committed activists continued their struggle to right an historical injustice committed by the Canadian government.

Reactions to the apology and redress agreement

After the House of Commons and Canadian Senate passed Bill C-331, *Internment of Persons of Ukrainian Origin Recognition Act*, spokespersons for the Ukrainian Canadian community stated,

> This represents a good will gesture and a very important step in securing recognition and reconciliation (to restore good relations) for the wrongs done to Ukrainians and other Europeans during this country's first national internment operations of 1914–1920, when thousands of men, women and children were needlessly imprisoned as "enemy aliens," had their wealth confiscated, were forced to do heavy labour, disenfranchised and subjected to other State-sanctioned censures.[1]

Speaking of those who endured the internment, Dr. Luciuk, then Director of Research, Ukrainian Canadian Civil Liberties Association said,

> We did not break [lose] faith. A score of years ago our community began to recover the memory of what it had endured—a "national humiliation," as an editorial writer described our disenfranchisement [loss of rights] in Canada's oldest newspaper, Kingston's *Daily British Whig*—one that sooner or later would have to be atoned [to repair or make up for] for. That time for atonement begins here, today, in Regina, with the first steps we now take forward together, having signed this agreement in principle that puts us on the path to securing an acknowledgement of an historic injustice, and so heralds [opens] the way toward reconciliation and a healing. And it does more, for it signals to all that, forever more, we are no longer "in fear of the barbed wire fence," and never again will be.[2]

However, despite the progress, spokespersons for the Ukrainian Canadian Congress felt there was more to be done:

> We look forward to the next step in the fall where we anticipate concluding a final agreement that will provide a proper acknowledgement and a series of commemorative, educational and community building initiatives.[3]

[1] Andrew Hladyshevsky, Paul Grod, and Lubomyr Luciuk, "Ukrainian Canadian leaders hail agreement." *The Ukrainian Weekly,* No. 36. September 4, 2005, p. 4.
[2] Lubomyr Luciuk, *Without Just Cause: Canada's First National Internment Operations and the Ukrainian Canadians, 1914–1920.* Kingston: Kashtan Press, 2006.
[3] Andrew Hladyshevsky, Paul Grod, and Lubomyr Luciuk, "Ukrainian Canadian leaders hail agreement." *The Ukrainian Weekly*, No 36. September 4, 2005, p. 4.

The following is a transcript of Bill C-331, *Internment of Persons of Ukrainian Origin Recognition Act*, assented to on November 25, 2005.

Internment of Persons of Ukrainian Origin Recognition Act

An Act to acknowledge that persons of Ukrainian origin were interned in Canada during the First World War and to provide for recognition of this event

Preamble

WHEREAS, during the First World War, persons of Ukrainian origin were interned in Canada under the authority of an Act of Parliament;

WHEREAS Parliament wishes to express its deep sorrow for those events;

AND WHEREAS Parliament acknowledges that those events are deserving of recognition through public education and the promotion of the shared values of multiculturalism, inclusion and mutual respect;

NOW, THEREFORE, Her Majesty, by and with the advice and consent of the Senate and House of Commons of Canada, enacts as follows:

Short title	1.	This Act may be cited as the *Internment of Persons of Ukrainian Origin Recognition Act*.
Negotiations	2.	The Government of Canada shall undertake negotiations with the Ukrainian Canadian Congress, the Ukrainian Canadian Civil Liberties Association and the Ukrainian Canadian Foundation of Taras Shevchenko towards an agreement concerning measures that may be taken to recognize the internment of persons of Ukrainian origin in Canada during the First World War.
Objective	2.1	The measures shall have as their objective a better public understanding of (a) the consequences of ethnic, religious or racial intolerance and discrimination; and (b) the important role of the Canadian *Charter of Rights and Freedoms* in the respect and promotion of the values it reflects and the rights and freedoms it guarantees.
Commemorative plaques	2.2	The measures may include the installation of commemorative plaques at certain places where persons of Ukrainian origin were interned in Canada during the First World War.
Public education measures	3.	The measures may also include the following public education measures: (a) the exhibition of information concerning internment camps and the contribution made by persons of Ukrainian origin to the development of Canada; and (b) the preparation of related educational materials.
Commemorative postage stamps	4.	The Government of Canada and the Ukrainian Canadian Congress, the Ukrainian Canadian Civil Liberties Association and the Ukrainian Canadian Foundation of Taras Shevchenko may request the Canada Post Corporation to issue a commemorative stamp or set of stamps.
Other commemorative measures	5.	The Government of Canada and the Ukrainian Canadian Congress, the Ukrainian Canadian Civil Liberties Association and the Ukrainian Canadian Foundation of Taras Shevchenko may consider any other measure that promotes the objective described in section 2.1.
Interpretation	6.	Negotiations undertaken pursuant to section 2 shall not be interpreted as constituting an admission by Her Majesty in right of Canada of the existence of any legal obligation of Her Majesty in right of Canada to any person.

Background to Japanese internment

Historical context

During the late 1800s, many young Japanese men left lives of extreme poverty in Japan in search of a better future. Some ended up in Canada, mostly on the west coast, only to face new hardships and an unwelcoming society. Many were already skilled fishermen in Japan and a few found work in the fishing industry on the west coast, either in the boats or at one of the dozens of canneries where the fish were processed and canned. Many others found seasonal work in other natural resource industries such as logging and mining, which were hungry for cheap labour. As the number of Japanese immigrants to Canada grew in the early 20th century, the phrase "Asian invasion" became widely used in the media, along with the term "yellow peril." Citizens of British Columbia, who were already angry with the growing Chinese immigrant population, saw the Japanese as an additional threat to their jobs and culture.

No. 1 – IMPOUNDED VESSELS AT ANNIEVILLE DYKE, FRASER RIVER PRIOR TO
RECONDITIONING FOR SALE.

Impounded Japanese Canadian fishing vessels at Annieville Dyke on the Fraser River in the early 1940s.
Source: University of British Columbia Library, Rare Books and Special Collections, JCPC 12b.001.

On September 10, 1939, Canada, a loyal British dominion, followed Britain's decision and declared war on Germany. Allied with Canada's enemies, Germany and Italy, Japan had attacked countries in Southeast Asia. As a result, Japanese Canadians came under increasing suspicion and their loyalty to Canada began to be questioned.

Details about Japanese internment

Immediately following Japan's attack on Hawaii's Pearl Harbor in December 1941, Canada, like its ally, the United States, declared war on Japan. The *War Measures Act* was passed, making every Japanese person in Canada, regardless of where they were born and whether they were a citizen of Canada or not, an enemy alien. Following the attack on Pearl Harbor, the lives of Japanese Canadians changed dramatically. Many lost their jobs, their fishing boats were seized, and Japanese cultural organizations and newspapers were closed. Curfews were imposed, and a "secure zone" that excluded Japanese men, was set up along the west coast.

Of the over 23,000 Japanese in Canada at the time, more than 75% were Canadian citizens. All were labeled enemy aliens. Local newspapers and radio stations continuously reported that Japanese spies were in their communities and would help the enemy when they invaded. In early 1942, the Canadian government ordered Japanese families to leave their homes and evacuate BC's coast. They were sent to internment camps in the province's interior and were permitted to bring with them only what they could carry. As the evacuation continued, the government began to take the possessions and belongings of Japanese Canadians. Cars were impounded and businesses and their contents were seized. The government took land, homes and their contents, as well as any other possessions that could not be carried in suitcases. In January 1943, an Order-in-Council was approved by the Canadian government requiring that all of the property be sold.

Women and children were sent to a variety of camps, most separated from their husbands and fathers. Men were sent to remote locations in the BC interior to perform forced labour. Living conditions in the camps were harsh, and the pay was well below subsistence level (what is needed to survive). Japanese Canadians who were interned lost their dignity and freedom.

Dining hall at the Slocan internment camp, British Columbia.
Source: University of British Columbia Library, Rare Books and Special Collections, JCPC 17.005.

In early 1945, when the end of the war was near, many politicians pushed for the Japanese to be deported from Canada. Those that stayed in BC during the war and chose not to go back to Japan were strongly encouraged to move east of the Rocky Mountains once the war was over. Going back to the BC coast was not an option. Some internees who had gone to the Prairies chose to stay there, while others left for areas farther east, including Ontario, Quebec and the Maritimes. About 13,000 Japanese Canadians decided to go east. Less than one third of the original Japanese population remained in BC.

Significance of Japanese internment

When the *War Measures Act* was lifted in December 1945, several thousand Japanese Canadians returned to the BC coast to start again, but they could never recover what was lost. Not only were their homes and businesses gone, but also their communities had been widely dispersed (separated). Although the war ended in 1945, discrimination against Japanese Canadians continued. Along with First Nations people, they were not allowed to vote in BC until 1949.

The internment of Japanese Canadians exposed the deep-rooted anti-Asian feelings in Canada in general and in BC in particular. Already a disenfranchised (lacking rights) minority group despite their efforts to adopt Canadian customs, the branding of Japanese Canadians as enemy aliens and the subsequent hardship and humiliation of internment left a painful imprint on the community. More than just an isolated incident, Japanese internment during World War II marks a deliberate and legally sanctioned policy by the Canadian government to take away the rights and property of a group of Canadians based on their race and country of origin/ancestry.

6.6ᴀ Response to Japanese internment

The movement for redress and early government responses

Protesters supporting the redressing of wrongs done to World War II Japanese internment victims in front of Canada's parliament buildings.

One of the Canadian government's first efforts to redress (make up for) the wrongs done to Japanese Canadians was to pay them back for their losses during World War II. In 1950, Justice Henry Bird recommended that individuals should receive $1.2 million compensation, but that their legal fees should be deducted from this amount. This amounted to $52.00 a person. While some individuals accepted this offer, most did not even file claims. For the next 20 years, there were no further compensation protests.

In the 1970s, the government allowed public access to government files. This allowed members of the public to review the government's wartime actions. Despite the fact that they were labeled "enemy aliens," it was revealed that the Japanese in Canada were never a threat to national security. In fact, documents indicated that the government's wartime actions were motivated by anti-Asian fears and the racist feelings of that period. Documents also showed that the war provided the government with an opportunity to respond to what was referred to as the "Japanese problem." The wrongs of the past were being exposed and could no longer be denied.

The year 1977 marked the100th anniversary of the arrival of Manzo Nagano, the first Japanese immigrant to Canada. During this year, the contributions of Japanese Canadians to Canadian society were highlighted. However, the injustices suffered by the Japanese during the war years were also revealed. As a result, the seeds for a redress campaign to be headed by the National Association of Japanese Canadians (NAJC) were planted. Eleven long years of struggle that included countless meetings, broken promises, disagreements within the Japanese community, rallies and protests, rejected proposals, public pressure, and an American government settlement for Japanese Americans, finally resulted in an agreement between the NAJC and the government of Prime Minister Brian Mulroney.

Government apology and the redress agreement

Official signing of the Japanese Canadian Redress Agreement by Prime Minister Brian Mulroney and Art Miki of the National Association of Japanese Canadians.
Source: 25th Anniversary of the Japanese Canadian Redress Agreement, Canadian Race Relations Foundation.

In his remarks to the House of Commons on September 22, 1988, Prime Minister Brian Mulroney officially apologized to Japanese Canadians for their internment during World War II. He stated,

> I know that I speak for Members on all sides of the House today in offering to Japanese Canadians the formal and sincere apology of this Parliament for those past injustices against them, against their families, and against their heritage, and our solemn commitment and undertaking to Canadians of every origin that such violations will never again in this country be countenanced or repeated.

On that day, the Japanese Canadian Redress Agreement was also signed. It consisted of:

- $21,000 for each individual Japanese Canadian who had been either expelled from the (west) coast in 1942 or was alive in Canada before April 1, 1949 and remained alive at the time of the signing of the agreement;

- a community fund of $12 million to rebuild the infrastructure of the destroyed communities;

- pardons for those wrongfully convicted of disobeying orders under the *War Measures Act*;

- recognition of the Canadian citizenship of those wrongfully deported to Japan and their descendants; and

- funding of $24 million for a Canadian Race Relations Foundation that supports projects, programs and conferences that promotes racial equality.[1]

Reactions to the apology and redress agreement

The following is a sample of responses to the Canadian government's apology and redress agreement from prominent members of the Japanese Canadian community.

On September 22, 1988, Canada's Judo King, Mas Takahashi, said on Parliament Hill,

> I feel I've just had a tumour removed.[2]

---

[1] "Japanese Canadians," *The Canadian Encyclopedias* http://www.thecanadianencyclopedia.ca/en/article/japanese-canadians/.

[2] Art Miki, "A need for vigilance" National Association of Japanese Canadians.

Writer Arthur Miki said,

> As I listened to the carefully chosen words of the Prime Minister's speech announcing the Redress
> Agreement negotiated with the National Association of Japanese Canadians (NAJC), memories of
> the five years of the redress campaign flashed through my mind—the struggle within the Japanese
> Canadian community, the struggle with the Government and five successive Ministers of State
> for Multiculturalism, and the struggle to win the approval of the Canadian public. The redress
> issue became a test for all of us who were involved in the NAJC. Would we be able to take and
> maintain a strong position on redress, and would we be able to persist until our goal of a "just and
> honourable" settlement was achieved?[3]

Albert Lo, chairperson of the Canadian Race Relations Foundation remarked,

> The Japanese Canadian Redress Agreement represents a milestone in the history of our country,
> in which the human rights violations Canada committed in the past were acknowledged... It
> constituted a model on which other Redress Agreements with Chinese Canadians, Aboriginal
> peoples who attended Residential Schools, and affected communities acknowledged through this
> Government's Community Historical Recognition Programme, have built... The celebration of
> this remarkable achievement allows us to continue to remember the past and to acknowledge the
> historical injustices and racism which were sanctioned [allowed] by the state.[4]

Mickey Nakashima, member of the British Columbia Japanese Canadian Citizens' Association, reflects on
what it meant to the Japanese community when he said,

> The acknowledgement, apology and symbolic compensation to those who were eligible and still
> living meant that the burden of shame and presumed guilt that *issei* [Japanese term for the first
> Japanese immigrants to North America] and *nisei* [Japanese term for the children of the first
> Japanese immigrants to North American] had carried for years was lifted. We were finally absolved
> of [freed from] any wrongdoing. The greatest regret was for the *issei* of my parents' generation who
> had died without witnessing Redress.[5]

---

[3] Roy Miki and Cassandra Kobayashi, *Justice in Our Time: The Japanese Canadian Redress Settlement*. Vancouver: Talon Books, 1991.

[4] 25th Anniversary of the Japanese Canadian Redress Agreement, Canadian Race Relations Foundation.

[5] Pamela Hickman and Masako Fukawa, *Righting Canada's Wrongs: Japanese Canadian Internment in the Second World War* Toronto: Lorimer, 2012.

6.7A Background to Chinese head tax

Historical context

Cartoon published in the April 26, 1879 *Canadian Illustrated News* showing Amor de Cosmos, a journalist and politician (who served as the second premier of British Columbia) and a Chinese immigrant.
Source: Charles Hou and Cynthia Hou, *Great Canadian Political Cartoons, 1820 to 1914*, (Toronto, ON: Moody's Lookout Press, 1997), p. 35.

The first large influx of Chinese immigrants to Canada originated in San Francisco. These immigrants came north to the Fraser River valley in British Columbia in 1858, following the gold rush. In the 1860s, many moved on to prospect for gold in the Cariboo Mountains in the interior of BC. The next large migration took place when the Canadian government allowed Chinese workers to immigrate to Canada in order to work building the Canadian Pacific Railway. Many were brought directly to Canada from China. These workers were expected to work longer hours for lower wages than their non-Chinese counterparts. From 1880 to 1885 about 17,000 Chinese labourers helped build the most difficult and dangerous British Columbia section of the railway, resulting in many deaths. In spite of their contributions, there was a great deal of prejudice against the Chinese. Some Canadian workers began to believe that the Chinese immigrant workers were a threat to their jobs and began to pressure the Canadian government to restrict further Chinese immigration.

Details about the head tax

When the railway was finished and cheap labour in large numbers was no longer needed, there was a backlash (negative reaction) from unionized workers and some politicians against the Chinese. In response, the Canadian federal government passed the *Chinese Immigration Act* in 1885. It imposed a tax of $50 on each Chinese person wishing to immigrate in the hopes of discouraging them from entering Canada. In 1900, the head tax was increased to $100. In 1903, the head tax rose to $500, which was equal to two years' pay.

During World War I, more Chinese workers were needed in Canada, resulting in an increase in Chinese immigration. After the war ended there was a backlash towards the Chinese from soldiers returning from the war looking for jobs. Also, many Canadians disliked the fact that the Chinese had begun to own land and farms.

Head tax certificate for Lee Don, 1918.
Source: Vancouver Public Library VPL 30625.

Significance of the head tax

According to a United Nations report, between 1885 and 1923, the Canadian government collected approximately $23 million through the head tax, which amounts to an estimated $1.2 billion in 21st century dollars. This represented a large source of revenue for the British Columbia and federal governments over a four-decade period. The tax was applied only to the Chinese, causing financial difficulties for many new immigrants.

The tax on Chinese Canadians exposed deep-seated anti-Asian feelings in Canada in general, and in British Columbia in particular. The head tax reinforced the outsider status of the Chinese and created great financial obstacles that led to many hardships for new immigrant families. The head tax reflects a deliberate policy of the Canadian government to keep out a group of immigrants based on their race and country of origin. As such, it is an example of a legally sanctioned injustice that unfairly targeted a group of Canadians.

6.8A Response to Chinese head tax

The movement for redress and early government responses

Head tax survivors and their spouses show their certificates during the struggle to obtain redress.
Source: John Bonnar, "New book details experiences of Chinese Head Tax families," *Rabble*, September 27, 2012.

The movement to redress (to make up for past injustices) the wrongs committed against the Chinese can be traced back to 1984. Vancouver Member of Parliament (MP) Margaret Mitchell raised the issue in the House of Commons of repaying the Chinese head tax to two people who lived in her riding. This encouraged 4,000 other head tax payers and their family members to seek representation by the Chinese Canadian National Council (CCNC), an organization that advocates for Chinese Canadians in their struggle to obtain redress from the Canadian government.

In 1993 Conservative Prime Minister Brian Mulroney offered individual medallions, a museum wing, and other measures to many other communities seeking redress for past wrongs. Chinese Canadian national groups felt this was inadequate and rejected the prime minister's offering outright. The same year, Jean Chrétien replaced Mulroney as prime minister, but his new Liberal government did not provide an apology or redress. However, the CCNC and its supporters did not end their struggle. They even raised the issue at the United Nations Human Rights Commission and eventually took the issue to court. They argued that the federal government should not profit from racism and that under the Canadian *Charter of Rights and Freedoms* and international human rights law it had a responsibility to redress this historical injustice.

In 1988, the apology and compensation for the internment of Japanese Canadians during World War II set the stage for redressing other racially motivated policies. By the time Paul Martin was appointed prime minister in 2003, it had become clear that there were perhaps only a few dozen surviving Chinese head tax payers still alive and likely only a few hundred spouses or widows. As a result, several national events were organized to strengthen the redress campaign. For example, in 2005, Gim Wong, the 82-year-old son of two head tax payers and a World War II veteran, conducted a cross-country "Ride for Redress" on his Harley Davidson motorcycle.

Prime Minister Stephen Harper delivers an apology for the head tax in the House of Commons.
Source: Office of the Prime Minister, Government of Canada.

Government apology and redress agreement

It wasn't until 121 years after the first head tax was placed on Chinese entering Canada that Canada officially recognized this historical wrongdoing. With intense pressure and perseverance from Chinese Canadian community organizations and individuals (the first Chinese Canadian filed a claim in 1983 to have the amount of the head tax returned to him), a settlement was finally reached in 2006.

On June 22, 2006 Stephen Harper, prime minister of Canada, offered an apology and compensation for the head tax paid by Chinese immigrants. Survivors or their spouses were paid approximately $20,000 in compensation. As of 2013, $16-million in compensation payments had been made. In 2008, the government of Canada devoted five million dollars to Chinese Canadian projects aimed at educating Canadians about discriminatory immigration restrictions applied in Canada.

Reactions to the apology and redress agreement

There have been mixed reactions to the redress agreement among Chinese Canadian. Some say the fight for redress is over while others say the compensation is not enough, given the suffering caused by the head tax. Some members of the community say the payments are not true compensation.

Colleen Hua, national president of the CCNC, said in a news release:

> This is a restorative [healing] moment for the Chinese Canadian community as we begin a genuine process of reconciliation [bring back friendly relations] with the Canadian government.[1]

An 88-year-old head tax payer, James Pon, expressed his satisfaction:

> I am grateful that I lived to see this day after so many years of trying to get the Canadian government to say "sorry."

Others in the community said the apology and settlement were not enough. This is revealed in the following excerpts from the *Globe and Mail*, published on Wednesday, June 30, 2010.

---

[1] Ottawa issues head tax redress payments to Chinese Canadians, CBC News (posted October 20, 2006).

Canada's apology to the Chinese community for the head tax from 1885 to 1923 was not enough, say descendants of those who paid the tax.

Ottawa said sorry to the Chinese community four years ago and gave $20,000 to those who had paid the head tax or to their surviving spouse.

But members of the Head Tax Families Society of Canada say the federal government excluded thousands of Chinese families who were affected by the historic injustices and Ottawa should rethink its approach to redress.

. . . The federal government acknowledged less than 1% of families who had paid the head tax, he said. Payments were made to about 800 people although more than 82,000 Chinese immigrants paid the tax from 1885 to 1923.[2]

Victor Wong, executive director of the Chinese Canadian National Council said:

For an apology to be meaningful, it needs to include the children of head tax payers.

In 2013 Jason Kenney, Minister for Citizenship, Immigration and Multiculturalism, celebrated the end of the five-year educational project. It was later revealed that $500,000 of the $5 million destined for Chinese Canadian projects had not been spent. However, the Canadian government took back the unspent money despite claims from Chinese Canadians that this was unfair.[3]

Transcript of the official government apology
Address by Prime Minister Stephen Harper of Canada on the Chinese Head Tax Redress

Ottawa, 22 June 2006

Mr. Speaker, I rise today to formally turn the page on an unfortunate period in Canada's past.

One during which a group of people—who only sought to build a better life—was repeatedly and deliberately singled out for unjust treatment.

I speak, of course, of the head tax that was imposed on Chinese immigrants to this country, as well as the other restrictive measures that followed.

The Canada we know today would not exist were it not for the efforts of the Chinese labourers who began to arrive in the mid-nineteenth century.

Almost exclusively young men, these immigrants made the difficult decision to leave their families behind in order to pursue opportunities in a country halfway around the world they called "gold mountain."

Beginning in 1881, over 15,000 of these Chinese pioneers became involved in the most important nation-building enterprise in Canadian history—the construction of the Canadian Pacific Railway.

From the shores of the St. Lawrence, across the seemingly endless expanses of shield and prairie, climbing the majestic Rockies, and cutting through the rugged terrain of British Columbia, this transcontinental link was the ribbon of steel that bound our fledgling country together.

It was an engineering feat—one for which the back-breaking toil of Chinese labourers was largely responsible—that was instrumental to the settlement of the West and the subsequent development of the Canadian economy.

The conditions under which these men worked were at best harsh, and at times impossible: tragically, some one thousand Chinese labourers died building the CPR.

. . .

---

[2] Robert Matas, "Head tax redress was not enough" *The Globe and Mail* (published online Wednesday, June 30 2010).

[3] Robert Matas, "Head tax redress was not enough" *The Globe and Mail* (published online Wednesday, June 30 2010).

But in spite of it all, these Chinese immigrants persevered, and in doing so, helped to ensure the future of Canada.

But from the moment that the railway was completed, Canada turned its back on these men. Beginning with the *Chinese Immigration Act* of 1885, a head tax of $50 was imposed on Chinese newcomers in an attempt to deter immigration.

Not content with the tax's effect, the government subsequently raised the amount to $100 in 1900, and then to $500—the equivalent of two years' wages—in 1903. This tax remained in place until 1923, when the government amended the *Chinese Immigration Act* and effectively banned most Chinese immigrants until 1947.

Similar legislation existed in the Dominion of Newfoundland, which also imposed a head tax between 1906 and 1949, when Newfoundland joined Confederation.

The Government of Canada recognizes the stigma and exclusion experienced by the Chinese as a result. We acknowledge the high cost of the head tax meant many family members were left behind in China, never to be reunited, or that families lived apart and, in some cases, in poverty, for many years. We also recognize that our failure to truly acknowledge these historical injustices has led many in the community from seeing themselves as fully Canadian.

Therefore, Mr. Speaker, on behalf of all Canadians and the Government of Canada, we offer a full apology to Chinese Canadians for the head tax and express our deepest sorrow for the subsequent exclusion of Chinese immigrants.

Gar nar dai doe heem.

This apology is not about liability today: it is about reconciliation with those who endured such hardship, and the broader Chinese-Canadian community—one that continues to make such an invaluable contribution to our great country.

And while Canadian courts have ruled that the head tax, and immigration prohibition, were legally authorized, we fully accept the moral responsibility to acknowledge these shameful policies of our past.

For over six decades, these race-based financial measures, aimed solely at the Chinese, were implemented with deliberation by the Canadian state.

This was a grave injustice, and one we are morally obligated to acknowledge.

To give substantial meaning to today's apology, the Government of Canada will offer symbolic payments to living head tax payers and living spouses of deceased payers.

In addition, we will establish funds to help finance community projects aimed at acknowledging the impact of past wartime measures and immigration restrictions on ethno-cultural communities.

No country is perfect. Like all countries, Canada has made mistakes in its past, and we realize that. Canadians, however, are a good and just people, acting when we've committed wrong.

And even though the head tax—a product of a profoundly different time—lies far in our past, we feel compelled to right this historic wrong for the simple reason that it is the decent thing to do, a characteristic to be found at the core of the Canadian soul.

Mr. Speaker, in closing, let me assure the House that this government will continually strive to ensure that similar unjust practices are never allowed to happen again.

We have the collective responsibility to build a country based firmly on the notion of equality of opportunity, regardless of one's race or ethnic origin.

Our deep sorrow over the racist actions of our past will nourish our unwavering commitment to build a better future for all Canadians.

Thank you.

6.9ᴀ Background to the *Komagata Maru* incident

Historical context

At the turn of the twentieth century, over two-and-a-half million people arrived in Canada during a period historians refer to as the first great wave of immigration. However, not all newcomers were welcome, and many experienced harsh treatment, discrimination and exclusion. For example, in western Canada, many Canadians felt that the growing number of immigrants from India would take over their jobs in factories, mills and lumberyards. As anti-Asian immigration sentiment grew, many western Canadians wanted the "brown invasion" to stop.

The *Komagata Maru* and its stranded passengers from India.
Source: City of Vancouver Archives. Item number CVA 7-125.

Pressure was put on steamship companies by the Canadian government to stop selling tickets to Indians. In 1907, a bill was passed denying all Indians the right to vote. The province of British Columbia began to pass strict laws discouraging the immigration of Indians to Canada. Indians had to have at least $200 in their possession to enter British Columbia and had to have come directly from India, without stopping at other ports along the way. With such obstacles in place to restrict the entry and integration of Indians into Canadian society, the stage was set for an explosive incident like the one that befell the passengers on board the *Komagata Maru*.

Details about the *Komagata Maru* incident

As a way to deny entry into Canada of those labeled "undesirable" immigrants, restrictive laws and regulations were passed. The most severe restriction to curb Indian immigration to Canada was the passage in 1908 of the *Continuous Passage Regulation* by the Canadian government. This law stated that immigrants must "come from the country of their birth, or citizenship, by a continuous journey and with tickets purchased before leaving the country of their birth, or citizenship." On May 23, 1914, a crowded ship from Hong Kong carrying 376 passengers, most of whom were immigrants from the northern state of Punjab in India, arrived in Vancouver's Burrard Inlet on the west coast of Canada.

Crowded deck of *Komagata Maru*, 1914.
Source: Vancouver Public Library, accession number 6232.

The passengers on the *Komagata Maru* were in violation of the *Continuous Passage Regulation*. As a result, the ship was prevented from docking by the port authorities. Passengers, who remained on board the ship for over two months, experienced severe hardships. The conditions on the boat quickly deteriorated and became unsafe. Passengers lost whatever money they had paid to take the journey. Only twenty Canadian residents returning to Canada and the ship's doctor and his family were eventually allowed to stay in Canada. The ship was escorted out of the harbour by the Canadian military on July 23, 1914 and forced to sail back to India.

Significance of the *Komagata Maru* incident

The *Komagata Maru* incident exposed the deep-rooted anti-Asian/Indian feelings in Canada in general and in BC in particular. The incident reinforced the outsider status of those who had immigrated from India. As a result, they faced greater obstacles to creating a life for themselves and their families in Canada. More than just an isolated incident, the plight of the passengers on the *Komagata Maru* reflects the deliberate, exclusionary policy of the Canadian government meant to keep out newcomers based on their race and/or country of origin.

6.10A Response to the *Komagata Maru* incident

The movement for redress and early government responses

Jaswinder Singh Toor, the president of the Descendants of the Komagata Maru Society, a leading organization that pushed for redress from the federal government.
Source: Jason Payne/PNG.

In 2006, the government of Canada responded to calls to redress (make up for past wrongs) historical injustices involving immigration and wartime discrimination. A program was created to fund projects for communities linked to unfair wartime practices and immigration restrictions. The announcement was made on June 23, 2006. This coincided with Prime Minister Stephen Harper's apology in the House of Commons for the Chinese head tax. On August 6, 2006, Prime Minister Harper made a speech at the Ghadri Babiyan da Mela (an Indo-Canadian community festival) in Surrey, BC, where he stated that the government of Canada was aware that the *Komagata Maru* incident was wrong and that the government was committed to discussing with the Indo-Canadian community how best to recognize this tragic episode in Canada's history.

Increased pressure put on government from Indo-Canadian community groups to go beyond words and to take action led other politicians to take up the struggle to obtain redress. On April 3, 2008, Ruby Dhalla, MP for Brampton-Springdale, introduced a motion in the House of Commons which read "That, in the opinion of the House, the government should officially apologize to the Indo-Canadian community and to the individuals impacted in the 1914 *Komagata Maru* incident, in which passengers were prevented from landing in Canada." Following further debate on May 15, 2008, the House of Commons passed Dhalla's motion.

On August 3, 2008, Prime Minister Stephen Harper apologized for the *Komagata Maru* incident at the 13th annual Ghadri Babiyan Da Mela in Surrey, BC.

On May 10, 2008, Jason Kenney, Secretary of State (for Multiculturalism and Canadian Identity) offered $2.5 million in grants and funding to recognize the *Komagata Maru* incident. These grants were available to members of the Indo-Canadian community to develop projects and initiatives that would honour those who experienced injustice as a result of the incident.

The unveiling of a memorial that recognizes the hardships suffered by passengers on the *Komagata Maru*.
Source: Komagata Maru Memorial Helps Heal Century-old Wounds, *Metro*, July 23, 2012.

Reactions to the apology and redress agreement

In response to the prime minister's historic apology, Jack Uppal, one of the most recognized and highly respected figures in Canada's Indo-Canadian community, said:

> Under the leadership of this Prime Minister, this government apologized for the historic injustice of the *Komagata Maru*. That apology was given in my house, my backyard, the place where the incident took place. I accepted the apology; the matter of an apology is closed. The *Komagata Maru* was a tragic incident in Canada's history, but this government has made remarkable efforts to right the wrong. From the Prime Minister's public apology, to the Minister of Immigration's establishment of the Komagata Maru Canadian historical recognition program, which has funded a significant number of educational projects, museums and memorials across the country, this government is to be commended for its approach to reconciling [correcting] a dark stain in our history.[1]

However, on Sunday, August 3, 2008, the Canadian Press announced "Sikhs don't accept apology for *Komagata Maru*." The article went on to say:

> Prime Minister Stephen Harper apologized Sunday for the 1914 *Komagata Maru* incident in which hundreds of Indians seeking a better life in Canada were turned away. Mr. Harper was speaking to a crowd of about 8,000 people in Surrey, BC, which has a large East Indian community. But as soon as he left the stage, members of the Sikh community rushed to the podium immediately denouncing the apology. They said they wanted it delivered on the floor of the House of Commons.[2]

Jaswinder Singh Toor, president of the Descendants of the Komagata Maru Society, said:

> The apology was unacceptable … We were expecting the prime minister of Canada to do the right thing. The right thing was … like the Chinese head tax [referring to Mr. Harper's full apology to the Chinese-Canadian community in 2006 for the head tax imposed on Chinese immigrants].[3]

Following Mr. Harper's speech, Sikh community leaders asked the crowd for a show of hands on whether or not to accept the apology. Then they announced that the gathering had rejected it. "The apology has been given

1   Cited by Tim Uppal, Minister of State, House of Commons Debates, *Hansard*, May 18, 2012.
2   Jeremy Hainsworth, Sikhs don't accept apology for *Komagata Maru*, *The Canadian Press*, August 3, 2008.
3   Harper Apologizes in B.C. for 1914 *Komagata Maru* Incident, CBC News (posted August 3, 2008).

and it won't be repeated," said Secretary of State Jason Kenney, who was accompanying Mr. Harper during his visit.[4]

Government apology and the redress agreement

Prime Minister Stephen Harper's federal apology for the 1914 Komagata Maru incident

Good afternoon, *Bonne après-midi (good afternoon), Sat Sri Akaal (a greeting used by Sikhs), Nameste (hello in Hindi), As-Salāmu Alaykum (a greeting used by Muslims)*. Thank you, Jason, for that introduction. Greetings to my colleagues, Nina Grewal, Jim Abbot, and Russ Heaper, and fellow Canadians. I'd like to begin today by thanking the president of the Mohan Singh Memorial Foundation, Sahib Thind, for inviting me once again to this spectacular showcase of Punjabi culture. The vibrant dance and musical traditions, exquisite art and timeless literature being celebrated here today are the fruits of a millennial old civilization whose influence spans the globe. Canada now shares this rich cultural legacy; it has become an integral part of our own cultural diversity. [French translation] Today over one million Canadians are of South Asian descent. These hard-working men and women passionately devoted to their families and communities are helping make our country even stronger for the generations yet to come, our country that affords opportunity to all, regardless of their background, our country that offers sanctuary to victims of violence and persecution, our country of freedom and democracy, of prosperity and peace, second to none in the world. As Canadians we have before us, and before our children and grandchildren, a future of literally unlimited possibility. A lot of that promise stems from the confidence, the ideas, and the energies brought here by successive waves of newcomers drawn to our shores by the promise of a new and better life. Canada is renowned the world over for its welcoming embrace of immigrants. But like all countries, our record isn't perfect. We haven't always lived up to our own ideals. One such failure, as has been mentioned, was the detention and turning away of the *Komagata Maru* in 1914, an event that caused much hardship for its passengers, 376 subjects of the British crown from Punjab, and which for many of them ended in terrible tragedy. Two years ago, I stood before you and made a commitment and since then, we have acted on that.

This May the Government of Canada secured passage of the unanimous motion in the House of Commons recognizing the *Komagata Maru* tragedy and apologizing to those who were directly affected. Today, on behalf of the Government of Canada. [Harper pauses to drink water]. Today, on behalf of the Government of Canada, I am officially conveying as Prime Minister that apology. Now friends, many Canadians have worked long and hard to secure recognition for this historic event. I'd like to thank from this community, the Professor Mohan Singh Foundation, the Khalsa Diwan Society, the *Komagata Maru* Descendants Association, and Community Leader, Tarlok Sablok, for their persistent and passionate dedication to this issue over the years. I also wish to acknowledge, I also wish to acknowledge my own colleagues, Nina and Gurmant Grewal, Parliamentary Secretary Jim Abbot, and Minister Jason Kenney for the work they have done to help all Canadians come to terms with this sad chapter in our history. We cannot change the events of the past; we cannot undo the misdeeds committed against those long deceased. But we can bring Canadians together in the present to unite our country, and to set us on a course to accomplish greater things in the future. In closing, I'd like to once again thank the organizers of this event for inviting me to once again be part of this tremendous festival. One of the most rewarding things about being Prime Minister is being able to travel across our great country and to meet the hard-working men and women of all faiths and cultures who are making Canada such a success. We should all be proud of our country and of each other and work together to build an even stronger Canada for all of us. Please enjoy the rest of the festivities. Thank you. *Merci beaucoup*. God bless our land.

---

[4] Harper Apologizes in B.C. for 1914 *Komagata Maru* Incident, CBC News (posted August 3, 2008).

6.11ᴀ Background to residential schools

Historical context

Before 1500 CE, Aboriginal societies in the Americas and societies in Europe developed separately from one and were largely unaware of one another's existence. Encounters between Aboriginal and non-Aboriginal peoples began to increase in the 1500s. Early contact was largely characterized by:

- mutual interest and curiosity;
- gradual increase in the exchange of goods;
- barter, trade deals, friendships, intermarriage, all of which created bonds between individuals and families;
- military and trade alliances, which encouraged bonds between and among nations.

While the early relationship between Aboriginal and non-Aboriginal peoples was more or less equal, this began to change in the 1800s. As the number of settlers increased, their power began to grow. As European settlers dominated the land, they also began to dominate its original inhabitants. Colonial and Canadian governments established reserves of land for Aboriginal people. Sometimes without treaty arrangements, these reserves generally lacked adequate resources and were often small in size. Increasingly, European settlers in Canada brought with them the belief that their own civilization was superior and had reached the pinnacle (height) of human achievement. They began to believe that the cultural differences between themselves and Aboriginal peoples proved that European civilization was superior, and that it was the responsibility of Europeans to provide guidance to the "ignorant and child-like savages." In other words, they felt the need to "civilize" the Aboriginal peoples. Education became the primary strategy to achieve this goal. Canada's first prime minister, Sir John A. Macdonald, advocated a policy of "aggressive civilization" which led to public funding for the residential school system.

Residential school students taking part in a class in penmanship at the Red Deer Industrial School (1914 or 1919).
Source: "Looking Unto Jesus." United Church of Canada, Archives, 93.049P/850N.

Details about residential schools

In 1849, the first of what would become a network of residential schools for Aboriginal children was opened in Alderville, Ontario. Church and government leaders concluded that the problem of "Aboriginal savagery" needed to be solved. This would be done by taking children from their families and communities at an early age, and teaching them the culture of the dominant society during eight or nine years of residential schooling. The main goal of the residential school system was to assimilate (absorb) and integrate Aboriginal people into Canadian society.

These photos portray the words of one government official who said that the residential school system was designed "to kill the Indian in the child."

Thomas Moore before and after his entrance into the Regina Indian Residential School in Saskatchewan in 1874.
Source: Library and Archives Canada / NL-022474.

With the passage of the *Indian Act* in 1876, residential schools became active. The federal government and churches operated over 130 residential schools across Canada. Attendance at residential schools was mandatory for Aboriginal children across Canada. Parents could be punished (and even imprisoned) for not sending children to these schools. Children were placed in schools far away from their parents and communities as part of a strategy to alienate (separate) them from their families and culture. Many Aboriginal children were taken from their homes by force. Those that attended residential schools near their communities were only occasionally allowed to visit their families, if at all. Students were not permitted to speak their language or practise their culture. If they did, they were often severely punished for doing so. There was a lack of nutritious food and many students were forced to do manual labour. Survivors of residential schools have reported that they experienced sexual and mental abuse, beatings and severe punishments. Overcrowded living conditions were common and children were forced to sleep outside in winter. Some reported cruel and inhumane punishments such as forcing children to wear soiled underwear on their head. Students suffered diseases and, in some cases, died while in residential schools. The last federally administered residential school was not closed until 1996.

Significance of residential schools

There were 132 federally-supported residential schools across Canada. This number does not include residential schools that were administered by provincial/territorial governments and churches. Approximately 80,000 survivors of these schools are alive today. As indicated by various statements of apology issued by the churches and by the Canadian government, students received a sub-standard education and most suffered extremely negative experiences.

In many cases, the abuses, and hardships associated with attending residential school have caused impacts such as post-traumatic stress disorder. Many survivors have struggled to engage in family, social and professional activities. Being away from their parents for long periods of time, survivors were not able to discover and learn valuable parenting skills. Taking children from their homes meant that transmission of language and culture was denied. As a result, many Aboriginal people no longer speak their native languages or are aware of their traditional cultural practices. Abusive behaviours learned from residential school have resulted in a cycle of abuse and trauma passed from one generation to the next. As a result, Aboriginal communities continue to experience some of the highest rates of substance abuse, violence, crime, disease and suicide in Canada.

Response to residential schools

The movement for redress and early government responses

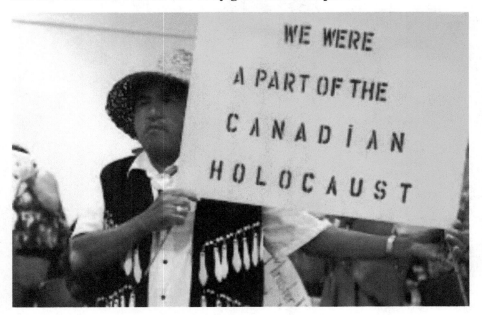

A residential school survivor celebrated the historic class action lawsuit to seek redress for abuses.
Source David P. Ball, *The Tyee*.

Until recently, the history of neglect and abuse in residential schools was largely unknown in Canada. Beginning in the late 1980s, Aboriginal groups filed lawsuits demanding compensation from the federal government for residential school abuse. This continued in the early 1990s, when Aboriginal leaders began to speak about their own experiences of violation at the schools. Only after this pressure did the Canadian government and churches begin to confront the issue. The possibility of a lawsuit that might result in a large settlement was also crucial in motivating a government response.

As a result of growing social problems in Aboriginal communities throughout Canada, in the early 1990s the federal government created the Royal Commission on Aboriginal Peoples (RCAP). This commission reported that residential schools played a large role in creating a social crisis in Aboriginal communities, and that the schools had left a legacy of trauma on generations of Aboriginal peoples. In response, the federal government created the Aboriginal Healing Foundation (AHF) in 1998. The AHF supports initiatives to help heal the scars left from physical and sexual abuse suffered in residential schools.

Government apology and the redress agreement

Following many years of work by survivors, Aboriginal communities and organizations, the government of Canada implemented the Indian Residential School Settlement Agreement (IRSSA) in September 2007. The following is a summary of the main elements:

- *Common Experience Payment* (CEP) set aside $40 million to pay eligible former students of residential schools up to $3000 each which they can use to further their education.

- *Independent Assessment Process* (IAP) is an out-of-court process to resolve claims of sexual abuse, serious physical abuse and other wrongful acts suffered at residential schools.

- *Truth and Reconciliation Commission* (TRC) was established to inform all Canadians about what happened in residential schools and their impact on the survivors, their families and communities. Over the course of

National Chief of the Assembly of First Nations Phil Fontaine accepting Canada's official apology for residential schools in the House of Commons on June 11, 2008.
Source: Prime Minister of Canada Stephen Harper, Government of Canada.

its five-year program, the TRC will provide former students and anyone affected by the residential school legacy with an opportunity to share their individual experiences in a safe and culturally appropriate manner.

- A $20 million initiative that supports local, regional and national activities that honour, educate, remember, memorialize and/or pay tribute to residential school students, their families and their communities.

- Indian Residential Schools Resolution Health Support Program (IRSRHSP) provides mental health and emotional supports for eligible former students and their families as they participate in the components of the Settlement Agreement.

- As part of the Settlement Agreement, the government of Canada provided $125 million to the AHF to support community-based healing initiatives.

In June 2008, the federal government apologized for its role in the residential school system. By saying he was sorry on behalf of the government, Prime Minister Stephen Harper acknowledged the Canadian government's central role in carrying out this historical injustice, and in inflicting untold pain and suffering on generations of Aboriginal children. Harper called residential schools a "sad chapter" in Canadian history and indicated that the policies that supported and protected the system were harmful and wrong.

Reactions to the apology and redress agreement

Assembly of First Nations (a leading political organization) National Chief Phil Fontaine stated in his acceptance of the government's apology,

> . . . for all of the generations which have preceded us, this day testifies to nothing less than the achievement of the impossible.

> . . . We heard the Government of Canada take full responsibility for this dreadful chapter in our shared history. We heard the Prime Minister declare that this will never happen again. Finally, we heard Canada say it is sorry.

. . . The memories of residential schools sometimes cut like merciless knives at our souls. This day will help us to put that pain behind us.

. . . I reach out to all Canadians today in this spirit of reconciliation—Meegwetch [thank you].[1]

First Nations abuse survivor Charlie Thompson, who watched the apology from the House of Commons gallery said he felt relieved to hear the prime minister acknowledge the horrible legacy.

Today I feel relief. I feel good. For me, this is a historical day.[2]

Inuit Tapiriit Kanatami (Inuit political and cultural association) President Mary Simon said,

I am one of these people that have dreamed for this day and there have been times in this long journey when I despaired that this would never happen. I am filled with hope and compassion for my fellow aboriginal Canadians. There is much hard work to be done. We need the help and support of all thoughtful Canadians and our governments to rebuild strong healthy families and communities. This can only be achieved when dignity, confidence and respect for traditional values and human rights once again become part of our daily lives and are mirrored in our relationships with governments and other Canadians.[3]

Native Women's Association of Canada President Beverly Jacobs said,

Prior to the residential schools system, prior to colonization, the women in our communities were very well respected and honoured for the role that they have in our communities as being the life givers, being the caretakers of the spirit that we bring to mother earth. We have been given those responsibilities to look after our children and to bring that spirit into this physical world. Residential schools caused so much harm to that respect and to that honour. We have given thanks to you for your apology. I have to also give you credit for standing up. I did not see any other governments before today come forward and apologize, so I do thank you for that.[4]

Tom King, Canadian author, Governor General's Award nominee and survivor of a U.S. residential school, said:

It is a symbolic act and it is really in the end no more than that. It is not going to change the history that we have had to live with and that many people will have to deal with. It is not going to change the damage that was done to native families, to reserves, to tribes across Canada. Today is just one day. What I am looking forward to is what tomorrow brings.[5]

Most believe there is still much to be done. Grand Chief Edward John of the First Nations Summit, an umbrella group of B.C, said,

The full story of the residential school system's impact on our people has yet to be told.[6]

---

1 Transcript of Chief Phil Fontaine (National Chief of the Assembly of First Nations), Aboriginal Affairs and Northern Development Canada, Government of Canada.

2 About Residential Schools, Legacy of Hope Foundation.

3 Transcript: Day of Apology, Aboriginal Affairs and Northern Development Canada, Government of Canada.

4 Transcript: Day of Apology, Aboriginal Affairs and Northern Development Canada, Government of Canada.

5 Reaction to the federal government's apology to Canada's Aboriginal People for the residential school system. Canwest News Service, June 11, 2008.

6 About Residential Schools, Legacy of Hope Foundation.

Apology delivered by Prime Minister Stephen Harper on June 11, 2008 in the House of Commons

Mr. Speaker, I stand before you today to offer an apology to former students of Indian residential schools. The treatment of children in Indian residential schools is a sad chapter in our history. In the 1870's, the federal government, partly in order to meet its obligation to educate aboriginal children, began to play a role in the development and administration of these schools.

Two primary objectives of the residential schools system were to remove and isolate children from the influence of their homes, families, traditions and cultures, and to assimilate them into the dominant culture. These objectives were based on the assumption that aboriginal cultures and spiritual beliefs were inferior and unequal. Indeed, some sought, as it was infamously said, "to kill the Indian in the child." Today, we recognize that this policy of assimilation was wrong, has caused great harm, and has no place in our country. Most schools were operated as "joint ventures" with Anglican, Catholic, Presbyterian or United Churches.

The government of Canada built an educational system in which very young children were often forcibly removed from their homes, often taken far from their communities. Many were inadequately fed, clothed and housed. All were deprived of the care and nurturing of their parents, grandparents and communities. First Nations, Inuit and Métis languages and cultural practices were prohibited in these schools. Tragically, some of these children died while attending residential schools and others never returned home. The government now recognizes that the consequences of the Indian residential schools policy were profoundly negative and that this policy has had a lasting and damaging impact on aboriginal culture, heritage and language.

6.13 Comparing official responses

Injustice	Summary of the historic injustice and consequences	Summary of offical response	Positive aspects of the official response	Shortcomings of the official response

Elements	Rating of actual response					Possible improvements
Public apology	+2 Reason:	+1	just right	-1	-2	
Compensation for victims and relatives	+2 Reason:	+1	just right	-1	-2	
Fact-finding about the event	+2 Reason:	+1	just right	-1	-2	
Preventative measures	+2 Reason:	+1	just right	-1	-2	
Public education	+2 Reason:	+1	just right	-1	-2	
Other	+2 Reason:	+1	just right	-1	-2	
Other	+2 Reason:	+1	just right	-1	-2	

Assessing the critique of an official response

Names: _____

	Outstanding	Well developed	Competent	Underdeveloped
Relevant and important consequences	Identifies many relevant and important consequences of the injustice.	Identifies many relevant consequences of the injustice.	Identifies some relevant consequences of the injustice.	Identifies a few of the relevant consequences of the injustice.
Reasons/explanation for rating				
Reasons for and against	For each of the criteria, identifies and explains thoughtful reasons for and against the adequacy of the official response to the injustice.	For most of the criteria, identifies generally thoughtful reasons for and against the adequacy of the official response to the injustice.	For most of the criteria, identifies and explains reasons for and against the adequacy of the official response; but some thoughtful reasons are missing.	For some of the criteria, identifies and explains reasons for and against the adequacy of the official response; but important reasons are missing.
Reasons/explanation for rating				
Justified overall assessment	The overall assessment is very reasonable and clearly justified by the reasons provided.	The overall assessment is reasonable and well justified by the reasons provided.	The overall assessment is reasonable and somewhat justified by the reasons provided.	The overall assessment is reasonable but weakly justified by the reasons provided.
Reasons/explanation for rating				

Assessing the ratings and suggestions

Names: _____

	Outstanding	Well developed	Competent	Underdeveloped
Reasonable ratings of response and possible improvements	Each of the individual ratings and suggested improvements are very reasonable, given what is known about the official response and the actions taken to redress this injustice.	Most ratings and suggested improvements are generally reasonable, given what is known about the official response and the actions taken to redress this injustice.	Most ratings and suggested improvements are somewhat reasonable, given what is known about the official response and the actions taken to redress this injustice.	Very few of the ratings and suggested improvements are reasonable, given what is known about the official response and the actions taken to redress this injustice.
Reasons/explanation for rating				
Accurate, relevant, and comprehensive supporting evidence	The evidence in support of the ratings is accurate, clearly relevant, and comprehensively includes the important facts for each criterion.	The evidence in support of the ratings is accurate, relevant, and includes the most important facts for each criterion.	The evidence in support of the ratings is often accurate and relevant, and includes a few of the important facts for each criterion.	The evidence in support of the ratings is often inaccurate or irrelevant and omits the most important facts.
Reasons/explanation for rating				

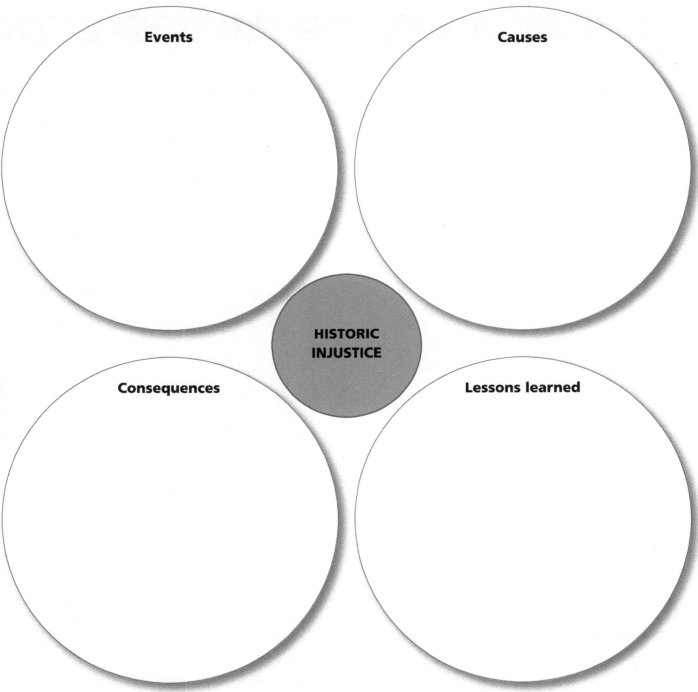

Events

Causes

HISTORIC INJUSTICE

Consequences

Lessons learned

Selection of key features of the event

The following features are the most **important, meaningful** (to those who experienced the event) and **helpful** (to ensure that history doesn't repeat itself).

Feature of the injustice	Reasons for choices
Events:	
Causes:	
Consequences:	
Lessons learned:	

Assessing the selection of key aspects

Names: _____

	Outstanding	**Well developed**	**Competent**	**Underdeveloped**
Relevant and accurate information	Suggestions are accurate and clearly relate to the four aspects.	Suggestions are generally accurate and relate to the four aspects.	Suggestions include some significant inaccuracies and do not always relate to the four aspects.	Suggestions are filled with inaccuracies or have little to do with the four aspects.
Reasons/explanation for rating				
Represent important aspects to remember	Selection represents a thorough understanding of the most important features of World War I internment to remember.	Selection represents a good understanding of the most important features of World War I internment to remember.	Selection represents an understanding of some of the important features of World War I internment to remember.	Selection suggests very little understanding of the important features of World War I internment.
Reasons/explanation for rating				

Judging the constitutionality of government actions

Government action	Would it infringe a *Charter* right?	Would it be a *reasonable limitation* of the right?		
		Prescribed by law	**Justified objective**	**Justified means**
Confiscation of property	**No** *The Charter of Rights and Freedoms does not specify rights over property.*	**Yes** *It was allowed by the War Measures Act.*	**Unsure** *I do not know how confiscating property might help keep Canada safe.*	**No** *Seizing property should not be pursued unless there is a clear objective.*
Arrest and detainment without trial				
Confiscation of literature including maps, photographs, letters				
Denial of ability to move around or leave the country				
Denial of citizenship				

Government action	Would it infringe a Charter right?	Would it be a *reasonable limitation* of the right?		
		Prescribed by law	Justified objective	Justified means
Denial of the right to vote				
Restraints of family, including children				
Forced labour and other camps				
Denial of humane treatment				
Retention after the war has ended				
Unequal treatment of various national and ethnic groups				

Determining *Charter of Rights and Freedoms* protections

Decide whether the following cases infringed the person's rights under the *Charter of Rights and Freedoms* and, if so, whether the conditions for reasonable limits were met.

Case 1: Mohammad Momin Khawaja

- Mohammad Momin Khawaja is a Canadian who was found guilty under the *Canadian Anti-Terrorism Act* in 2009.
- The law's objective is to prevent terrorist activity and was passed in December 2001 following the attacks on the US on September 11, 2001.
- Khawaja, a computer programmer, was arrested in 2004 and convicted in 2009 of financing and building remote control devices that could trigger bombs.
- Khawaja appealed the decision arguing that the section of the anti-terrorism law that states that terrorist activity is committed "in whole or in part for political, social, religious, or ideological purpose, objective or cause" is unconstitutional.
- Khawaha argued the law infringes upon his freedom of religion, freedom of association and freedom of expression.
- Khawaja argued that the law encourages law enforcement to scrutinize people based upon their religious, political and ideological beliefs.

The Supreme Court of Canada made its decision in 2012. Based upon the information given to you, how would you decide?

Explain which, if any, of Khawaja's *Charter* rights and freedoms were infringed upon?	If so, did the treatment of Khawaja meet the three conditions for reasonable limits?

Case 2: Yat Fung Albert Tse

- In 2006 the police were informed of an alleged kidnapping after family members began receiving phone calls demanding the payment of ransom.
- Without telling the family, police began an emergency wiretap of the phone under Section 184.4 of the *Criminal Code,* which allows for unauthorized wiretaps by any peace officer if the situation is urgent and harm may be done to an individual.
- The next day the police received judicial authorization (necessary for all wiretaps).
- The *Criminal Code* does not require that the police report on how often they used Section 184.4 and how often, after the fact, the courts rejected their use of the emergency provision.
- As a result of the wiretap evidence, Albert Tse and five others were arrested and charged with crimes relating to the alleged kidnapping.
- Tse appealed the decision, arguing that the emergency wiretap infringed his *Charter* rights.
- The Supreme Court of Canada had to decide if Section 184.4 of the *Criminal Code* was constitutional and whether its use in this case could be justified under Section 1 of the *Charter*.

The Supreme Court of Canada made its decision in 2012. Based upon the information given to you, how would you decide?

Explain which, if any, of Tse's *Charter* rights and freedoms were infringed upon?	If so, did the case of Tse meet the three conditions for reasonable limits?

Restricting government actions

Government action	Right or freedoms under the *Charter of Rights and Freedoms*	In what way could this government action be revised in order to make it constitutional? For each action you may wish to . . . • add more protection for certain groups or individuals; • remove an existing provision; or • limit use for certain circumstances. In some cases no revision may be possible. In this case, explain why.
Confiscation of property		
Arrest and detainment without trial		
Confiscation of literature including maps, photographs, letters		
Denial of ability to move around or leave the country		
Denial of citizenship		

Government action	Right or freedoms under the *Charter of Rights and Freedoms*	In what way could this government action be revised in order to make it constitutional? *For each action you may wish to . . .* • *add more protection for certain groups or individuals;* • *remove an existing provision; or* • *limit use for certain circumstances.* *In some cases no revision may be possible. In this case, explain why.*
Denial of the right to vote		
Restraints of family, including children		
Forced labour and other camps		
Denial of humane treatment		
Retention after the war has ended		
Unequal treatment of various national and ethnic groups		

Context of the World War I internment operations

World War I

- When the British Empire, alongside Russia and France, declared war against Germany, the Austro-Hungarian Empire and the Ottoman Empire in 1914, Canada was automatically at war.

- On August 22, 1914 the Canadian government led by Prime Minister Robert Borden passed the *War Measures Act* giving the government certain powers during times of war.

- Canada fought in World War I from 1914 until the armistice on November 11, 1918 (Remembrance Day) that ended the fighting.

- World War I officially came to an end with the signing of the final peace treaty in 1920; this officially ended the internment operation.

Enemy aliens

- The Canadian government was greatly worried about the hundreds of thousands of immigrants living in Canada who were citizens of such enemy nations as Austria-Hungary, Germany, Bulgaria and the Ottoman Empire.

- The government of Canada issued an Order-in-Council providing for the registration and, in certain cases, the imprisonment of aliens of "enemy nationality."

- An estimated 120,000 people living in Canada were designated as "enemy aliens" (citizens of a country at war with the land in which he or she is living).

- From August 4, 1914 to February 24, 1920, 80,000 individuals were forced to report regularly to special registrars or to local or North West Mounted Police forces. These individuals included Ukrainians, Bulgarians, Croatians, Czechs, Germans, Hungarians, Italians, Jews, various people from the Ottoman Empire, Polish, Romanians, Russians, Serbians, Slovaks and Slovenes, among others, of which most were Ukrainians and most were civilians. They were issued identity papers that had to be carried at all times, and those failing to do so could be subjected to arrest, fines or even imprisonment.

- Restrictions were also imposed on freedom of speech, association and movement of enemy aliens. Municipalities were told to watch all Germans and Austrians living within their areas, and all enemy aliens were prevented from leaving the country.

World War I internment operations

- In total, 8,579 enemy aliens (including 81 women and 156 children) were interned in 24 internment camps across Canada. The internment camps held 5,954 Austro-Hungarians (believed to be mostly Ukrainians), 2,009 Germans, 205 people from the Ottoman Empire and 99 Bulgarians.

- Throughout the war years, numerous letters, petitions and memoranda were addressed to the federal and provincial authorities by Ukrainian Canadian organizations, asserting that the Ukrainian Canadians were loyal to the Dominion of Canada and the British Empire, not Austria-Hungary.

- Although many camps closed from 1916 to 1918, camps in Vernon (British Columbia), Kapuskasing (Ontario) and Amherst (Nova Scotia) were not closed until 1919 or 1920, a full year and a half after the end of the war.

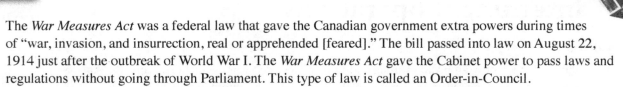

8.5 Overview of the *War Measures Act*

The *War Measures Act* was a federal law that gave the Canadian government extra powers during times of "war, invasion, and insurrection, real or apprehended [feared]." The bill passed into law on August 22, 1914 just after the outbreak of World War I. The *War Measures Act* gave the Cabinet power to pass laws and regulations without going through Parliament. This type of law is called an Order-in-Council.

The powers granted to Cabinet included the ability to pass laws and regulations "deemed necessary for security, defence, peace and welfare." More specifically, it granted the government power over the following:

a) censorship, control and forceful prevention of publications, writings, maps, plans, photographs, communications and means of communication;

b) arrest, detention, exclusion and deportation;

c) control of the harbours, ports and territorial waters of Canada and the movements of vessels;

d) transportation by land, air or water and the control of the transport of persons and things;

e) trading, exportation, importation, production and manufacture;

f) taking over without permission and disposing of property.

The *War Measures Act* was invoked three times during the 20th century in Canada.

World War I, 1914–1920

- The *Act* was first used was during World War I, until its official end in 1920 with the signing of the final treaty.

- It was used primarily to arrest and detain Canadians of Ukrainian, German, and Slavic descent who were considered "enemy aliens."

- An "enemy alien" was defined as a person living within Canada who descended from a nation or empire that Canada was at war with. In the case of World War I, this included Germany and countries that were part the Austro-Hungarian Empire.

World War II, 1939–1945

- During World War II, Canada invoked the *Act* again due to perceived threats from various groups of "enemy aliens."

- This included the arrest, internment, deportment and seizure of property of Canadians of Japanese, Italian and German descent.

The October Crisis, 1970

- The October Crisis was the only time the *War Measures Act* was invoked during peace time.

- The *Act* was invoked by the Liberal government of Pierre Trudeau in response to two kidnappings by the Front du Libération du Québec (FLQ).

- The *Act* was used to arrest and detain more than 450 people in Quebec who the government believed may have been part of an "armed insurrection."

When the *Emergencies Act* of 1988 was passed by Parliament, the *War Measures Act* was repealed. This new *Act* introduced changes that would force Cabinet to seek Parliament's approval, and for any laws passed to be subject to the *Charter of Rights and Freedoms*.

8.6 *Charter of Rights and Freedoms*

The Canadian *Charter of Rights and Freedoms* is entrenched within the Constitution, which means it is a permanent part of the Constitution and cannot be easily changed or ignored by any level of government in Canada.

The *Charter* defines the fundamental freedoms and rights of people in Canada and prohibits governmental officials and agencies from infringing upon the following rights and freedoms.

Fundamental freedoms (section 2)

- Freedom of conscience and religion
- Freedom of thought, belief, opinion and expression; and freedom of the press
- Freedom of peaceful assembly and association

Democratic rights (sections 3-5)

- Right for every citizen to vote
- Right to have elections at least every five years

Mobility rights (section 6)

- Right to enter, remain in, or leave Canada
- Right to live, work, or study in any province or territory in Canada

Legal rights (sections 7-14)

- Right to life, liberty, and security of person
- Secure from unreasonable search and seizure
- Right to not be arbitrarily arrested and detained
- Right to a fair trial if accused of a crime
- Right to receive humane treatment

Equality rights (section 15)

- Right not to be discriminated against on the grounds of race, national or ethnic origin, religion, sex, sexual orientation, age, mental or physical ability

Official languages of Canada (sections 16-22)

- Right to communicate and receive communication in French or English for any governmental service including the court system

Minority language education rights (section 23)

- Right to be educated in either French or English where sufficient numbers of students exist

Enforcement (section 24)

- Right to take the matter to court should any of the above rights and freedoms be denied

None of these right and freedoms are absolute, which means they may be overridden if there are strong reasons for doing so. Section 1 of the *Charter* contains a clause dealing with reasonable limits which explains the criteria that must be met to justify overriding the rights outlined in the *Charter*.

Section 1 of the *Charter of Rights and Freedoms* specifies that governments may be justified in placing limits on the rights protected by the *Charter* as long as certain conditions are met:

> The Canadian Charter of Rights and Freedoms *guarantees the rights and freedoms set out in it subject only to such reasonable limits prescribed by law as can be demonstrably justified in a free and democratic society.*

This means that *Charter* rights are not absolute. Even when a right has been infringed upon by a governmental authority, it may still not violate the *Charter* if there are good reasons for limiting the right. The task of applying these reasonable limits is a difficult one. The Supreme Court of Canada has interpreted "reasonable limits" and "demonstrably justified in a free and democratic society" to mean that limits on rights and freedoms may be permitted if three conditions are met:

Prescribed by law: To be *prescribed by law* a limit must be embodied in an existing law or authorized by a properly delegated official or agency. For example, a police officer cannot arbitrarily or inconsistently decide to infringe a *Charter* right without a valid law or authorized superior directing the officer to act in this way.

Clearly justified objective: The government's objective or goal in wanting to limit the right must be reasonable and clearly justified. The limitation must have sufficient merit or importance in order to justify overriding a constitutionally protected right. For example, the courts may decide that limiting a person's freedom of assembly is justified in order to safeguard public safety and protect life, but it may decide that limiting a person's freedom of assembly is not justified merely to avoid minor traffic delays.

Clearly justified means: The way or method used by the government to limit individual rights must also be justified. The Supreme Court has suggested three factors to consider in relation to the means:

- whether the means is carefully designed to achieve the objective;
- whether it interferes as little as possible with the right in question;
- whether it causes less harm than it avoids.

For example, police officers may be justified in encouraging a groups of people who are demonstrating to disperse for reasons of safety; but arresting the entire group for their safety may not be a justified means, since there may be less drastic ways to protect their safety.

The courts must first decide whether or not a right or freedom specified in the *Charter* has been infringed, and then consider all three conditions in deciding whether or not the infringement was a reasonable limitation of that right.

Changes to the *War Measures Act*

The *War Measures Act*, passed in 1914, has been amended a number of times, during times of war as well as peace. Following its use in the October Crisis of 1970, there was much criticism that the act granted too much power to the government. In 1988, the *War Measures Act* was replaced with a new law known as the *Emergencies Act*.

The *Emergencies Act*, 1988

The *Emergencies Act* retains many of the provisions in the *War Measures Act* to enable the government to act to maintain public order and national security in times of crisis, emergency or war. The main changes are added checks on government power. The *Emergencies Act* includes protections to prevent or limit overreaching government actions during war, emergency or internal crisis.

- All orders and regulations are subject to Parliamentary review. This means that Cabinet must seek the approval of Parliament and cannot act alone.

- Individuals who are negatively affected by the government during times of emergency may seek compensation.

- The government's actions are subject to the *Charter of Rights and Freedoms*. This provision acknowledges that rights and freedoms can be limited subject to Section 1, Reasonable Limits.

The *Anti-Terrorism Act*, 2001 and *Combatting Terrorism Act*, 2013

In 2001, following the September 11th attacks on the World Trade Center, the government of Canada passed a new anti-terrorism law designed to increase national security. Various provisions of this law lapsed (were cancelled) in 2007, in what are known as "sunset clauses." The *Combatting Terrorism Act* of 2013 renewed many of these provisions. This *act* grants law enforcement agencies the following powers:

- detainment of terror suspects for three days without charge;

- preventative detainment of someone suspected of committing a terror crime in the future;

- hold secret hearings (non public) for terror suspects;

- arrest of someone trying to leave the country for suspected reasons of terrorist activities;

- require individuals with knowledge of terror activities to disclose information or face prison if they do not;

- stiff penalties for harbouring, financing or training terrorists.

The above legislation can be amended or repealed by the government at any time. In any future crisis, war or emergency, the government has the power to introduce new legislation that could limit rights and freedoms; however, the *Charter of Rights and Freedoms* remains entrenched in the Constitution.

Assessing *Charter* conclusions

Names: _____

	Outstanding	**Well developed**	**Competent**	**Underdeveloped**
Identifies *Charter* rights	Identifies a very reasonable suggestion for the *Charter* right(s) that may be involved for every government action.	Identifies a very reasonable suggestion for the *Charter* right(s) that may be involved for almost every government action.	Identifies reasonable suggestions for the *Charter* right(s) that may be involved for most of the government actions.	Identifies very few reasonable suggestions for the *Charter* right(s) that may be involved with any of the government actions.
Reasons/explanation for rating				
Offers plausible conclusions about *Charter* implications	Provides very reasonable conclusions about the implications of the *Charter* for each government action.	Provides reasonable conclusions about the implications of the *Charter* for almost every government action.	Provides reasonable conclusions about the implications of the *Charter* for many government actions.	Provides few reasonable conclusions about the implications of the *Charter* for any of the government actions.
Reasons/explanation for rating				
Offers plausible restrictions on government actions	For each government action, provides a plausible restriction to make it conform with the *Charter* or explains why no change is needed.	For almost every government action, provides a generally plausible restriction to make it conform with the *Charter* or explains why no change is needed.	For many government actions, provides a generally plausible restriction to make it conform with the *Charter* or explains why no change is needed.	Provides few plausible restrictions to make the government actions conform with the *Charter* and offers few convincing explanations why no change is needed.
Reasons/explanation for rating				

Critiquing a commemorative display

Injustice to be memorialized: _____

What I know about the injustice

	Describe the aspects, feelings/ message and symbols/images	Explain what is effective about the display	Suggest what might be done to strengthen the display
Captures important aspects or details to educate the public about the event and its significance			
Sends a powerful message or feeling about the event			
Uses interesting symbols and images to represent the event			

World War I internment in Canada

Source: Canadian First World War Internment Recognition Fund

During Canada's first national internment operations of 1914–1920, thousands were branded "enemy aliens", transported to camps in the country's frontier hinterlands, and there forced to do heavy labour, not because of anything they had done wrong but only because of where they had come from and who they were.

Cambodian killing fields

Source: Keith Brooks

Source: John Campbell

The Killing Fields refers to the systematic murder of Cambodian civilians by the Khmer Rouge regime between 1975 and 1979. It is estimated that a quarter of the country's population was killed during this genocide.

Source: Polyanka Libid

The Great Famine of 1932–1933 in Soviet Ukraine which took the lives of many millions of Ukrainians is known as the Holodomor.

9.5 Canadian soldiers in World War I

Source: Graham MacKay

World War I (1914–1918) was monumental for Canadian identity. Many have suggested that Canada became an independent nation and began to be recognized internationally after the Great War.

Holocaust during World War II

Source: Florida Center for Instructional Technology

The Holocaust refers to the systematic extermination of European Jews and the mass murder of Roma, homosexuals, the disabled, Jehovah's Witnesses and political dissidents by Nazi Germany and its collaborators between 1941 and 1945. Many millions of Ukrainians, Poles, Russians and other Slavic people were also enslaved or murdered.

Rwandan genocide

Source: Radu Sigheti

The Rwandan genocide was the systematic slaughter of Rwandans of Tutsi descent by Hutu militants in 1994. Many felt the United Nations and the international community could have done more to prevent this atrocity.

Ranking the commemorative displays

Name of the injustice and type of commemorative	Important information or details	Strong message or feeling	Interesting symbols or images

The two most powerful commemorative displays based on the criteria are:

1.	Rationale
2.	Rationale

Names: _____

	Outstanding	Well developed	Competent	Underdeveloped
Understands the contents or message	Demonstrates excellent understanding of the memorial's contents or message.	Demonstrates a good understanding of the memorial's contents or message.	Demonstrates some understanding of the memorial's contents or message.	Shows no understanding of the memorial's contents or message.
Reasons/explanation for rating				
Identifies positive features	Thoughtfully identifies important positive features for each criterion.	Identifies some important positive features for each criterion.	Identifies a few positive features.	Does not identify any important positive features.
Reasons/explanation for rating				
Points out areas for improvement	Suggests insightful and relevant improvements to the commemorative display for all three criteria.	Suggests relevant improvements to the commemorative display for all three criteria.	Suggests a few improvements to the commemorative display.	Does not suggest any relevant improvements to the commemorative display.
Reasons/explanation for rating				

Assessing students' commemorative displays

Names: _____

	Outstanding	Well developed	Competent	Underdeveloped
Important aspects of the injustice	The most important aspects associated with the event, its causes, consequences and the lessons learned are represented in the commemorative.	Several important aspects associated with the event, its causes, consequences and the lessons learned, are represented in the commemorative.	Some important aspects of the injustice are represented in the commemorative.	Very few of the important or relevant aspects are represented in the commemorative.
Reasons/explanation for rating				
Powerful message or feelings	The commemorative communicates a very powerful message or feeling about the injustice.	The commemorative communicates a powerful message or feeling about the injustice.	The commemorative communicates a limited message or feeling about the injustice.	The commemorative does not communicate a clear message or feeling about the injustice.
Reasons/explanation for rating				
Interesting symbols and images	The commemorative includes a number of very interesting symbols and images to represent the event.	The commemorative includes some very interesting symbols and images to represent the event.	The commemorative includes some interesting symbols and images to represent the event.	The commemorative has very few interesting symbols and images.
Reasons/explanation for rating				

Advice on mural making

Use the following guide as a springboard to making a mural. Feel free to incorporate your own creative ideas. If you've never done a mural, start small. The size of the mural is not as important as the mural message and what you learn making it.

Murals are traditionally painted directly on walls, but moveable wood or canvas murals have several advantages over those painted on walls:

- wood panel or vinyl murals do not require school-site permission to paint. Even if you can't find a location or permission from your principal, you can still get started.

- wood /vinyl panel murals can be painted safely inside the classroom in a controlled environment.

- moveable murals can be permanently hung in awkward locations too high or dangerous for students to access safely and if the need ever arises, they can be moved to new locations.

Before starting, determine where the mural will be hung once it's finished. This is important to build not only student motivation, but it will also affect the mural design. The amount of small and large details will depend on how close the mural will be to its audience. Also, don't let the school be the only location for your mural. Preschools, social service agencies, senior centres, parks and local businesses are all potential sites for murals.

Rules for keeping paint where it should be

1. Stay in designated area.
2. Stay on plastic covered area.
3. Use one designated washroom for clean-up.
4. Wear shoe covers at all times when in the area.
5. Take shoe covers off to leave paint area—check shoes to make sure no footprints or paint spots get on floor.
6. Keep paint and brushes on an assigned table.
7. Keep brushes in colour pots designated to that colour to avoid muddying colours.
8. No paint should be taken into washrooms.
9. Prevent flushing of paint into the water system by using rubber or disposable gloves instead of rinsing paint-covered hands in the washroom.